YARN
Spinning
WITH A MODERN TWIST

Dedication

To all wool craft lovers past, present and future.

First published in 2023

Search Press Limited
Wellwood, North Farm Road,
Tunbridge Wells, Kent TN2 3DR

Text copyright © Vanessa Kroening, 2023

Photographs and design copyright
© Search Press Ltd., 2023

Photographs by Mark Davison

Photograph of monarch butterfly on page 46
by Alicia Kroening.

ISBN: 978-1-78221-794-7
eBook ISBN: 978-1-78126-751-6

The Publishers and author can accept no responsibility for
any consequences arising from the information, advice or
instructions given in this publication.

Suppliers
If you have difficulty in obtaining any of the materials and
equipment mentioned in this book, then please visit the
Search Press website for details of suppliers:
www.searchpress.com

You are invited to visit the author's website:
www.thespinnersstash.com

Acknowledgements

I would like to give special thanks to my husband, Nick, who
loves and supports me and my fibre obsession, and my
son, Jonah, who is always up for helping me with all of my
little woolly tasks and adventures. Thank you, Lizzette, for
being you and being there for me to help and encourage me
through the process of writing this book. And thank you to
all of my family and friends who stuck with me and cheered
me on through the entire duration of the book.

Thank you so much to Katie and May for recognizing the
potential of my work and suggesting I write a book about my
process. Thanks again, May, you were an absolute pleasure
to work with and you were there with me every step of the
way. Lastly, thank you to the entire Search Press team for
not only making this book possible, but making it more
beautiful than I ever could have imagined.

YARN
Spinning

WITH A MODERN TWIST

HOW TO CREATE YOUR OWN GORGEOUS
YARNS USING A DROP SPINDLE

VANESSA KROENING

SEARCH PRESS

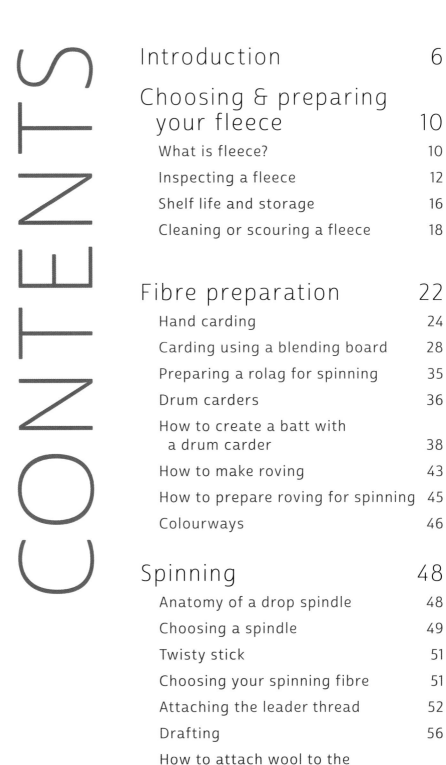

CONTENTS

Introduction 6

Choosing & preparing
your fleece 10

What is fleece? 10

Inspecting a fleece 12

Shelf life and storage 16

Cleaning or scouring a fleece 18

Fibre preparation 22

Hand carding 24

Carding using a blending board 28

Preparing a rolag for spinning 35

Drum carders 36

How to create a batt with
a drum carder 38

How to make roving 43

How to prepare roving for spinning 45

Colourways 46

Spinning 48

Anatomy of a drop spindle 48

Choosing a spindle 49

Twisty stick 51

Choosing your spinning fibre 51

Attaching the leader thread 52

Drafting 56

How to attach wool to the
leader thread 57

Spinning singles 60

Starting to spin 62

Plying 68

Lazy kate 68

Winding a centre-pull ball 69

Making a standard two-ply yarn 71

Andean plying 72

Finishing the yarn 75

Making a niddy noddy 80

Setting the twist 85

Drop spindle techniques 86

Basic thread plying 86

Autowrapping 87

Cloud spinning 88

Lock spinning 89

Core spinning 98

Using embellishments 102

Dyeing 110

How to dye fibre 111

Dip dyeing 112

Other dyeing methods 113

Yarn inspiration 114

Expanding your knowledge further 124

Glossary 126

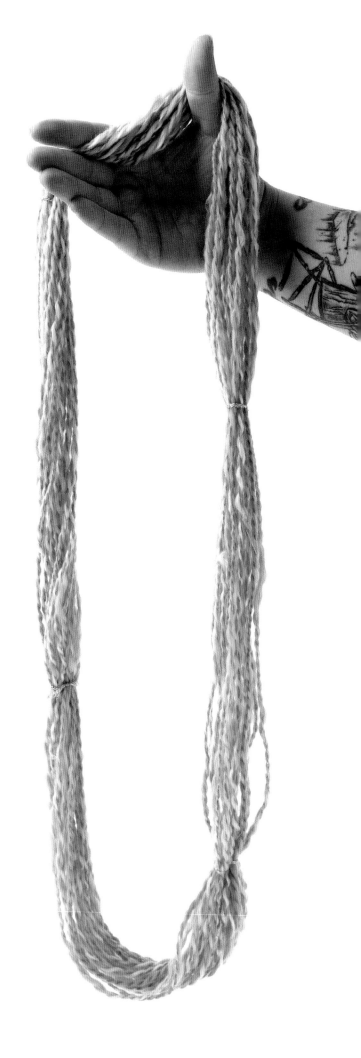

Introduction

This book is intended to inspire and educate you, whether you are a fibre artist or a lover of wool crafts, and to introduce you to the wonderful, colourful world of home fibre processing, spinning and creating.

When exhibiting at shows, I meet many people who are intrigued by the prospect of making their own yarn, but have no idea how to get started. Lots of them have their own supply of raw wool, but it goes to waste, partly because they lack the knowledge of how to process it and because many believe that making yarn is something that can only be accomplished by machines in factories. This book shows you that, not only is that not true, but it is quite easy and amazingly satisfying to do at home on your own – and you don't even need a spinning wheel!

Utilizing a drop spindle for spinning is an optimal way to begin your spinning journey. Drop spindles are quite easy to come by if you enjoy browsing the internet or attending wool shows (and, if you are super crafty, you can easily put together your own spindle, even if it is not perfect). Hand spinning is much cheaper than buying a spinning wheel, not to mention that a spindle is much smaller and far easier to store. In fact, a spindle is so compact you can carry it around town with you in your shopping bag or in a handbag.

Using a spindle slows down the spinning process and breaks it up into manageable steps. It is ideal if you only want to produce small quanitites of yarn, and it is the perfect introduction to the craft of spinning. Then, once you resign to the fact that you have become a spinning/fibre addict, you can take your obsession to the next level and begin checking out spinning wheels.

Although drop spinning is a traditional craft, there are many reasons – personal, economic or otherwise – that people may choose to do it. All that matters is that you are here, and you want to learn. Over the years, I have gained my knowledge of spinning through personal research, meeting like-minded people, sharing ideas and skills, and an extreme amount of trial and error. This book gathers together some of that knowledge and skill that I have acquired from all corners of the earth. Hopefully, this will ease you into the wonderful world of spinning with minor frustration and loads of great fun.

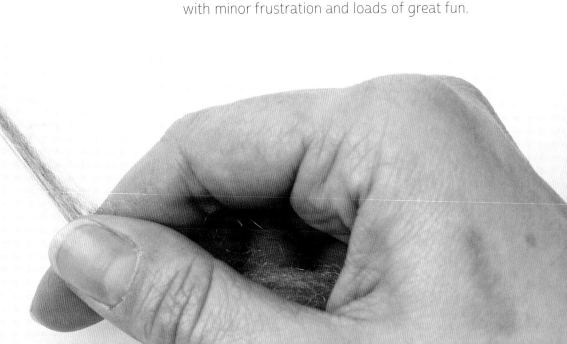

What's in this book?

You will discover the entire process, right from choosing your fleece, to storing your finished yarn.

❀ Choose a fleece – what to look for and how to assess its suitability, best use, colour, age and general condition (see pages 10–17).

❀ Clean and prepare your raw fleece and fibres (see pages 18–23).

❀ Blend colours and textures by hand and with various tools. I have also included a couple of dyeing techniques that I use on some of my fibres. It is always good to experiment with colour whether it is pre-dyed or you do it yourself (see pages 24–47 and 110–113).

❀ Choose and use your drop spindle (see pages 48–67).

❀ Discover some art yarn spinning techniques to make yummy yarn adorned with beads, sequins, locks, beehives and other quirky goodness (see pages 88–109).

❀ Ply your yarns using standard or Andean plying to bolster your yarns and make them stronger (see pages 68–74 and 86–87).

❀ Remove your gorgeous yarn from the spindle and set the twist so it doesn't become an unravelled, tangled mess (see pages 75–85).

❀ Discover what you can you do with your finished yarn in my Yarn Inspiration section (see pages 114–125). (Spoiler alert: you can do anything you want with it! If you spin your yarn with good structural integrity, you can utilize it just as you would any commercial yarn. I have used my hand-spun yarn as a standalone piece, in knitting, crochet, weaving, felting, dreamcatchers and countless other colourful creations.)

BE AWARE

For the purposes of photography I have occasionally parked and posed my yarns during the spinning process to show clearly what I'm doing – the angles may not represent how you would actually hold the thread while spinning, so ensure you read and reread the instructions before you start.

Choosing & preparing your fleece

What is fleece?

To begin, let's talk about fleece. A sheep's fleece is the wool that grows on its body in much the same way that human beings grow hair. A sheep's fleece is most commonly cut or 'sheared', to use the proper term, in the springtime. There are, however, some long-wool breeds that must be shorn twice a year and even some that don't require shearing at all.

Wool characteristics and properties can vary greatly between breeds and often even *within* the same breed. Wool from sheep is known as a 'protein fibre'. The fibres form microscopic barbs which point away from the base of the fibres. These barbs help the fibres to grab and stick to neighbouring fibres. This makes wool ideal for spinning and, with the help of temperature and agitation, good for felting as well. Think, for example, of that time you didn't check the washing instructions on that gorgeous wool jumper before loading it into the laundry and it came out the size of pixie clothes and was impossible to restore to its original state (of course I have never personally done this…).

Variances in wool can result in many different levels of fibre quality. To help determine the quality of wool you have or are going to purchase, you will want to know that for many spinners, quality = softness. One way the softness of wool is measured is by the diameter of the individual fibres. This measurement is then expressed in microns. The micron count can be especially helpful to give you an idea of the quality of wool you will be purchasing when buying wool online. The smaller the fibre, the lower the micron count. In general, the lower the micron count, the softer the wool. If all of this confuses you, don't worry, just trust your touch! Part of the spinning adventure is to seek out various breeds, work with the wool, and decide for yourself what you like.

In addition to sheep's wool, there are endless types of fibres that can be spun into yarn. I have spun with everything from alpaca to camel and flax to nettles. I have experimented with various synthetic fibres and even things such as newspaper and plastic bags. To report my findings on each material would take ages and I know you just want the abbreviated version so you can get spinning.

On the spectrum of sheep's wool, any advice included throughout is standard practice and suitable for most breeds, but not conclusive across the board. For the purposes of this book, when I refer to fibre, fleece or wool, I am referencing sheep's wool, unless otherwise stated.

Assortment of natural fleece from seven different sheep breeds, and a handmade drop spindle from The Spinner's Stash.

QUICK START

If you are overwhelmed by the idea of choosing, cleaning and preparing a fleece yourself, you can jump straight to spinning by purchasing wool tops, which have already been scoured, combed and sorted, or roving, which has been scoured and carded.

CAUTION

Fibre fondling can lead to extreme wool addiction!

Inspecting a fleece

When choosing a fleece, you will want to assess the quality and suitability of the wool for the project you have in mind. Take into account things such as intended use, colour, age, general condition, price and how much you will need.

First, carefully roll out the fleece onto a tarpaulin or any other flat surface so you can get a good look at the entire piece.

TIPS

* It is usually a red flag if the seller will not let you inspect the wool before purchase.

* Be sure to wear gloves if you are pregnant, breastfeeding, or have an allergy to lanolin.

Things to look for

Staple length: the staple is the average length of the individual fibres of the fleece.
To determine staple length, measure a lock of unstretched fibre from tip to butt.

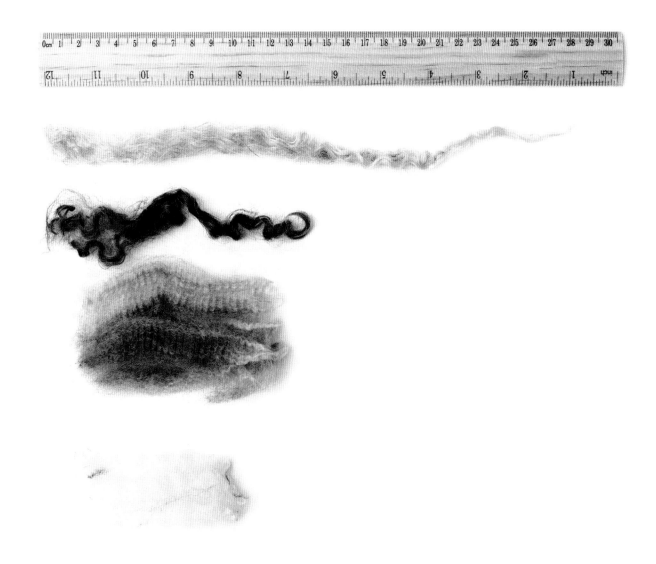

Noils and second cuts: this is when the shearer does not cut the fleece in one swipe and has to do another pass. This creates a break in the staple length, so instead of having one long fibre, you have two small ones. Second cuts can be spun, but are not ideal for a beginner.

Weathered/felted/matted: there are many things that wool in this condition may be used for, but spinning is not one of them. Pay particular attention to the shoulder and back-end areas. The shoulders are hard-wearing areas that get beaten down by weather... the back end is self-explanatory.

Crimp: this refers to the natural waves in individual fibres. The amount of crimp in fibres can affect your final project. I find that the more crimp there is, the fuller and bouncier the yarn is.

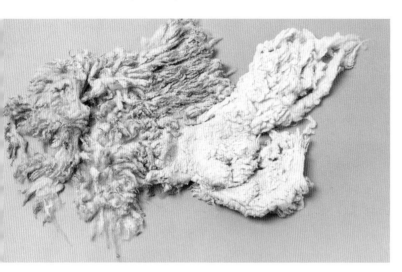
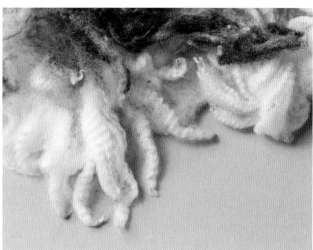

Kemp: these are weak, brittle fibres that may be present in a fleece. These will generally be peppered throughout the fleece and appear as the opposite colour of the overall fleece. Kemp can add wonderful character to a fleece, but you may find that it has some negative qualities such as coarseness and an inadequate ability to retain dye.

Lanolin: this is the natural grease produced by a sheep. Personal preference will dictate whether lanolin is removed during the cleaning process, or left in for spinning.

Stains: look for any stains or paint on the fleece. Pay particular attention to the back end of the fleece for urine stains as they are particularly hard to remove and can permanently damage the integrity of the fibres.

Breaks or tenderness: this refers to a weak spot in individual fibres that can indicate a sick sheep. To check for breaks, you can do the 'snap test'. Hold a lock of fibre with the butt in one hand and the top in the other. Give a quick tug to both sides of the wool. The wool should not break in two, but you should hear a soft, satisfying snap. Repeat this process a couple more times randomly over the length of the fleece. If the fleece fails the snap test, it is not a suitable fleece for spinning.

Vegetable matter: sheep live outdoors, so they will get dirty. You need to assess the amount of vegetable matter they have collected. Look for grass, hay, straw, burrs and other unwanted organic material. Keep in mind that you will be removing each and every piece, so if you are not willing to take the time to do that, then it is not worth buying the fleece.

Soiling: substances like poo and mud can usually be removed by cleaning, but make sure that you are willing to put in the work if the fleece happens to be heavily soiled.

Skirting: this is the removal of undesirable fibre and materials from the edges of the fleece. If you find that a fleece has not been skirted before purchase, ensure that you are not paying for the fleece by weight.

Colour: there is a wide range of beautiful natural colours, but if you are planning on dyeing your fleece, take note that darker colours will not take dye as well as lighter ones.

Purchasing a fleece: some great references that I always use when purchasing wool are the websites of the British Wool Board (www.britishwool.org.uk) and the American equivalent, Sheep USA (www.sheepusa.org).

On these sites you can research what the going rates are for wool and other pertinent information to sourcing and buying fleece. There is a wealth of knowledge to be gained by browsing these sites and countless links to related information. When researching different sheep breeds, their characteristics and even history, I always refer to what I like to call the 'fleece bible'. The book's real title is *The Fleece and Fibre Sourcebook* (published by Storey Publishing, 2011).

Shelf life and storage

The shelf life of a fleece is directly affected by how you store it. The ideal conditions are cool, dry and without insects or other unwanted creepy crawlies. Keep your fleece in the house or a properly insulated shed or outroom so that it is free from exposure to the elements.

If you are unable to store your wool in a cool, climate-controlled environment, make sure it is in a breathable bag to help prevent condensation or moisture buildup. Using a plastic bag or container may sound very sanitary and, it is true, you will get a lovely seal. However, if you live in a hot or humid climate, or you are planning on storing the containers in an environment that is not temperature controlled, you may run into issues with condensation. If your wool gets wet, it could lead to moulding or encourage insect infestation, which would most likely ruin your fleece.

A muslin cloth bag or a hessian potato sack are ideal because they are breathable, so if there is any residual dampness or condensation, it will be able to escape.

It is important that the fleece be, at a minimum, skirted (if not scoured/washed) before storage (see pages 18–21). Make sure you cinch the opening of the bag tightly to help prevent any insect infestation. You do not want to store your wool and forget about it forever. At a minimum you should inspect it once every three months. Do a once-over and keep a look out for mould, moisture and bugs. When you are digging through, it is a good idea to give the wool a good stir or shake to rotate the wool; I have heard that this can disturb any moth eggs that may have presented as well as give your wool a much-needed breather.

There are a number of methods, potions and general wizardry to assist in keeping your wool free from creepy crawlies. Moth balls are an obvious go-to in moth prevention; however, there is an offensive smell that tags along with them. I prefer the use of cedar wood or cedar balls that can be purchased on the internet quite easily if you cannot find them at a general store. There are also a number of sprays that can be purchased online that claim to repel moths and other insects from a various wools and other textiles. You will just have to research and experiment for yourself and find what works for you.

WARNING: A fleece's shelf life will be adversely affected if you store it when it is still wet, so make sure it is completely dry beforehand.

CARE INSTRUCTIONS

Just as with any wool garments or other assorted wool items, you must take special care when handling your fleece. Wool has a tendency to felt when not handled properly. Always be very careful when washing or treating your fleece and be mindful of the conditions that can cause felting.

Felting is basically when the individual wool fibres grab onto each other and squeeze for dear life. This creates a matted effect that cannot be easily undone, if at all. The key to felting (whether you are trying to felt or not) is rapid temperature change and agitation of fibres. Essentially, heat opens up the microscopic 'barbs' on individual fibres. Changing rapidly to cold will snap those barbs shut. Add some friction into the mix and it becomes a big tangled mess that binds together. If you are not actively seeking this outcome, I suggest you pay special attention to temperature and the amount of stroking taking place.

Aside from that, gentle hand washing in tepid water with a delicate or wool wash is best. While your wool is in the water, I suggest swishing in a forward and backward motion or swishing around in a circle to release any soiling. Do not squeeze or rub the fleece while washing. Once removed from the bath, you may then gently squeeze out excess water.

caution
Never wring out wool, as the friction may cause felting.

Examples of wool fleece packed in appropriate storage bags.

Cleaning or scouring a fleece

Cleaning your fleece properly and thoroughly is very important as it removes unpleasant substances, helps to remove harmful chemicals that the sheep may have been exposed to and enables the fibre to be processed further with additional ease. It is ultimately up to you what level of cleaning (also known as scouring) you would like to do.

With any luck, a purchased fleece will have already been skirted. Skirting is the process of removing the undesirable bits of the fleece. These sections can include very dirty spots around the rear end, heavily weathered or damaged fleece around the neck and underbelly, and areas that I like to call 'dirty beyond repair'. In the event that you encounter a fleece that has not been skirted, the task will be left up to you.

Prior to scouring, some people sometimes use what is called a 'duster' to assist in removal of vegetable matter. A duster is a big, barrel-shaped structure covered in chicken wire with a crank on the end. This contraption sits atop a stand that allows it to be rotated round and round like a clothes dryer. This tumbling action allows loose particles of unwanted material, such as dirt and vegetable matter, to shake loose and fall through the mesh. It is a really neat tool to have, but the cheaper version of this is to simply grab onto the edge of the fleece and give it several good shakes, turn it and do it again. You will notice that this can produce the same outcome as using a traditional duster with minimal extra effort. Continue to shake out your fleece until you fail to see foreign matter dropping out of it.

A lightly skirted raw fleece rolled for storage.

You will generally remove all damaged sections of fleece as well as those areas that have dye on them (see right).

How to clean your fleece

1 Do your best to remove all vegetable matter such as grass, leaves and straw. Don't worry if there are a few tiny pieces left behind, as these can still be removed later in the fibre preparation or during spinning.

2 Separate your fleece into piles ranging from heavily soiled to lightly soiled. By doing this, you can tailor the cleaning process for each batch of fibre.

3 Tease apart the fibres with your hands or use a picker (see page 23) to help you spot any undesirable materials and to open up compacted fibres to make way for the water to clean it.

4 To wash the fleece, you will need to find a suitable container that is deep enough for the wool to float in and not touch the bottom. The wool needs to float freely to enable the bits of debris to fall to the bottom of the container and away from the fleece. The container must also be wide enough that the fleece is in a thin layer; this way, the water can work its magic all the way through the fleece. I use an old galvanized bathtub, see right. You will also need some washing-up liquid or wool wash, some tongs and a potato masher.

Find an old container such as a galvanized bathtub (see above) to use for washing your fleeces.

On the left are teased fibres from the fleece on the right.

5 To prepare the wool bath, fill it with hot water (hot enough that you can bear to stick your hand in, not boiling) and approximately two tablespoons of washing-up liquid or your choice of wool wash. Follow the instructions on the bottle for your specific brand of wool wash. Add the wool after the water to assist with felting prevention.

6 Lower the fleece carefully and slowly into the water and let it soak for 15 minutes. Gently push the wool under the surface of the water to ensure it is completely submerged.

7 Refrain from poking, squeezing or touching the wool too much during washing to help prevent the fibres felting. A potato masher is good for pushing the fleece down, gently swirling and scooping it out of the bath. Metal tongs are also useful for lifting the fleece out of the water.

8 Make sure you don't let the water cool too much before removing the wool, as the lanolin that has melted down may reconstitute into clumps and settle back on the wool. If this happens it is very difficult, if not impossible, to get it out of the wool.

9 Remove the wool from the soap bath by gently squeezing excess water from the fibre and placing it in a fresh hot-water bath. Don't add any soap. Repeat this rinsing process with clean hot water as many times as it takes for the fleece to look clean and the water to run clear.

10 If you just want to remove the dirt but not the lanolin, then it is safe to fill the tub with tepid, rather than hot, water. It is fine to leave the wool in to soak for as long as you would like, but I recommend approximately an hour before removing the fleece and gently squeezing the water out. Then dump the water, rinse the tub and refill it with water of the same temperature and put the wool back in.

11 Remove the fleece from the water for the last time and gently squeeze out all the excess water. Take care not to agitate or wring the wool, as this may cause felting.

TIPS

* If you are planning on processing your fibre using a drum carder (see page 36), hand carder (see page 24) or a blending board (see page 28), it is a good idea to clean it first so it is easier to handle and does not damage your equipment.

* You may add a few drops of your favourite essential oil to the wash if you like.

DON'T...

...use your household tub or sink for the washing process, because not only is it pretty disgusting, but you also run the risk of getting sick or contaminating your household with sheep poo, chemicals and bacteria.

12 You can use a spin dryer (but with no heat) to remove excess water if you would like to accelerate the drying process. If you intend to do this, you will need to put the fleece into a mesh bag to prevent felting.

13 Lay the wool out to air dry. To ensure that it dries thoroughly, it is best to find something that will allow the air to circulate all around it. I use a mesh frame (see right). If the weather is dry, put the wool outside to help it dry.

14 While the wool is still slightly damp, pick through it again for remaining materials that shouldn't be there. Once the fleece is dry, pick through it again just to make sure you have removed all the yucky bits.

Your cleaned and dried fleece will look quite different from the fleece you started with! Make sure that it is completely dry before you store it. See page 16 for information on storage of fleece.

TIP
You may wish to leave the lanolin in your fleece so that you can 'spin in the grease'. Traditionally, spinning in the grease was more common than not and often preferred. Leaving lanolin in not only makes your hands super soft while spinning, but also helps to keep fibres more waterproof, which can be handy if your final project is to be an outer garment.

Clean and dry fleece.

Fibre preparation

So you have a clean fleece. Now what? The choice is yours. You can begin spinning your wool straight away or you can process it even further. Your batch of fibre can be used as a standalone yarn or it can be blended with other fibres to create a different look or texture or sent to the dye pot for additional colour variations.

There are countless ways to prepare your fibres for spinning. The tools that you choose to use (or perhaps not use) will greatly impact your final yarn. Here are a couple of methods to get you started, but remember, there are loads more tools out there.

Using your hands

1 Teasing wool apart with your hands is an excellent way to break up packed fibres or to mix different colours and textures together with ease and without tools. Using your hands also gives you greater control over the fibres. Grab a handful of fibre with both hands. Grip the edges of the fibres with a loose hold...

2 ...and pull the fibres away from each other.

3 Repeat this process until there are no clumps of fibre left or until you are satisfied with the texture.

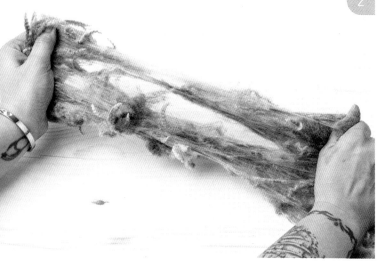

Using a box picker

Teasing the wool apart with your hands is a good, affordable option, but it can also be time-consuming and very tedious. When processing bigger quantities of wool, you may want to use what is called a picker.

There are two different types of picker: the box picker and the swing picker. The swing picker is an intimidating looking piece of kit (not to mention reminiscent of a medieval torture device); I avoid this one.

I prefer to use a box picker (see right). Always follow the manufacturer's instructions, but to give you the gist of it, the picker itself is a box-like structure with a series of nails pointing in strategic directions. It has a slider – a horizontal piece of wood with a handle – which sits atop and also has a generous number of nails in it. The slider is positioned on one end of the picker and a small amount of wool is placed on it. The slider is then pushed from front to back, racking the wool back and forth, separating and fluffing it up.

The majority of the wool will be pushed out of the other side once it has been picked. The remaining wool can then be carefully pulled from the picker as needed.

Using a wool flicker

Wool flickers are a great hand tool for opening up small quantities of fibres, or loosening the tips of locks. You can purchase a fancy flicker at a wool shop or online, but do not underestimate the power of a dog brush from your local pet store. A cheap brush will do just the same as an expensive one.

Use the brush on wool just as you would on tangled hair. Start at the tips and work your way up. Take notice of the name 'flicker', this is the technique you will use to open up the ends of your long wool fibres. Use a flick of the wrist when brushing beautifully long locks, do NOT brush the entire staple, just flick the tips. Doing it this way will open up the end of the long staple so it can be spun into the yarn easily, while keeping the gorgeous locks intact.

A typical pet brush purchased from an ordinary store can be used as a flicker on wool.

Combs and hackles

These are good tools for aligning long staple fibres to help make them smooth and easier to spin. Both tools can be held by hand or clamped to a table. Unlike with combs however, with a hackle (a board or strip with rows of upturned nails) you can stack colours and pull roving with a diz (an often disc-shaped item with width gauges cut into it, see right). You will want to use fibre that has already been brushed through with a comb to make it easier to lash onto the tines of the hackle.

Drawing fibre through a hole in a diz (shown) helps you draw a consistent width for spinning (see pages 43–44).

Hand carding

Hand carders are probably the most affordable tool for carding, although they are time-consuming and a lot of effort to use. Carding is better for short fibres; unlike combing or flicking, you do not have to hold the fibres with your hand while brushing.

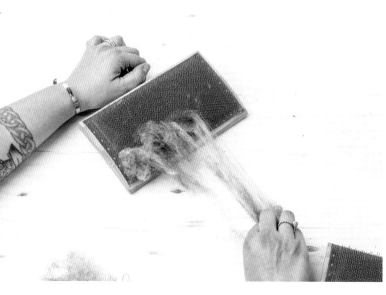

1 Lay one carder down on the table or your lap and load by dragging the fibres on against the tines in the opposite direction of the handle.

2 Fill with fibres from the bottom up, as shown in step 1, being careful not to overfill the tines. Once full, grip the left-hand carder and hold firmly.

3 Take the right-hand carder and place it with the tines down on top of your left-hand carder, with the handles facing in opposite directions. Drag the right-hand carder away from the left-hand carder with long strokes (keeping the left-hand carder still).

4 Continue until your fibre has mostly transferred from the left-hand carder to the right-hand carder.

5 Then you will repeat the process, this time passing it back to the original carder by switching the hand that is on top – so you will have the left-hand carder on top, making long strokes on the right-hand carder, which is now at the bottom.

6 Continue to switch back and forth, passing the fibres from hand to hand until any foreign matter is brushed out along with any knots or clumps of fibre. The fibre will begin to look more uniform as you go along. Keep going until you are satisfied with the consistency. If you are carding to blend colours or textures, continue the process until you are satisfied with the look and feel of it.

7 Now you need to start a process called 'doffing'. Place the right-hand carder on top of the left-hand carder with tines facing each other and handles lined up.

8 Now slowly pull the handles away from each other keeping the top of the carders engaged. This will pull the fibre into one big flat rectangle called a batt.

9 There are two simple ways I like to remove the batt from the hand carders. The first is to gently tug the fibre off the carder as one complete flat piece.

10 The second is to create a 'puni' – a neat roll pulled directly off the hand carders ready for spinning. Gently roll the fibre onto itself (this can be done with or without a pair of dowels, as shown here) and off the carder. To use dowels, place one under the fibres that overhang the bottom of the carder and the other on top. Pinch the dowels together, slide them down to the tip of the fibres and roll the dowels upwards, holding them together securely, to wrap the fibres around them.

11 Keep rolling it evenly to the top of the carder.

TIP

If you make a puni, you can spin it the same way as you would a rolag (see how to spin from a rolag, page 35).

12 Once you reach the top, you can remove it from the carder completely and then slide it off the dowels, one at a time (see steps 24–25 on page 32).

Your fleece will come off the dowel in a tube known as a puni and can be rolled into a neat spiral called a 'rolag' for safekeeping.

Carding using a blending board

A blending board is a wonderful tool for mixing colours and fibres. They vary in price but are generally an affordable way to take your spinning to the next level by creating and blending unique colourways with a variety of textures.

In this section we will use a blending board to make rolags. A rolag is a roll of fibre created by first adding the fibre to the blending board for carding and then by gently rolling it off the board. You can then use this wool to start spinning. If properly prepared, a rolag will be uniform in width, with evenly distributed fibres.

1 Position the board so that the tines are curved away from you.

2 Grip a handful of fibre loosely in one hand to make a long stroke down the blending board. Use the other hand as a guide for the fibres.

3 Space the fibres out to begin with, making sure you pull them down to the bottom.

4 Continue to load fibres across the blending board using this technique, taking care to distribute them evenly and adding in some different colours.

caution
Be careful, as the tines on a blending board are very sharp and can cause injury.

5 Gradually fill in the gaps until the board is covered.

6 You may want to add in some extra fibres to give additional texture (here I added some silk fibres).

7 Starting at the bottom right and about a third of the way up, use your brush to brush the fibres down. Brush from bottom to top.

8 Work your way across from right to left, just brushing the bottom third of the board.

9 Next, begin brushing two thirds of the way up and from right to left again.

10 You have now brushed the bottom two-thirds of the fibre.

11 Then start brushing the top third of the fibre. Do this carefully so as not to pull the fibre away from the board.

12 The brushing is completed.

13 If you wish, you can now begin to add accent fibres such as glittery Angelina or shiny viscose fibre in the same way as before.

14 Brush these in as you go.

15 Repeat the process of loading the fibre until the blending board is full, but do not overload the tines; only fill if you can still see shiny tines poking out.

16 Then brush the fibres again in the same way as before.

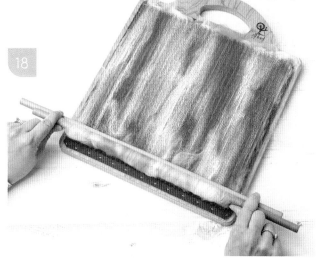

17 Now take two dowels, placing one under the fibres that overhang the bottom of the board and the other on top.

18 Pinch the dowels together, slide them down to the tip of the fibres and roll the dowels upwards, holding them together securely, to wrap the fibres around them.

19 Pull towards yourself firmly to 'draft' the fibres out a bit – this simply means drawing them out to a desired length while keeping them thick enough to work with (pay attention to the staple length – you do not want to draft further than that). See page 56 for more information on drafting.

20 Roll the fibres tightly around the dowels.

21 Repeat the drafting and rolling a couple more times until you are satisfied with the amount of fibre on your dowels.

22 When you are ready, pull the dowels completely away from the blending board to separate the fibres.

23 Incorporate any wispy fibres by lightly smoothing them round the dowels in the same direction as the other fibres.

24 Hold the dowels firmly in one hand. With the other hand, slide one of the dowels out of the roll. The dowel should slide out from the fibre smoothly without taking anything with it.

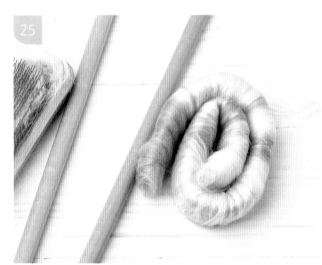

25 Pull the second dowel out. You will now be left with a gorgeous rolag.

26 You may need to tug or brush up the fibres to enable easy access for the dowels again.

27 Continue to remove fibre from the blending board using the same technique as before.

28 Wrap the fibre round the dowels, draft it and pull it as before.

29 Continue on to complete the second rolag.

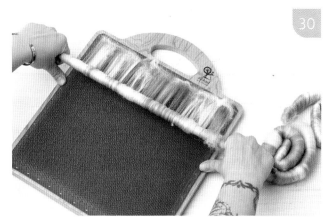

30 Keep going until you have used up all the fibres from the blending board. You should be able to get at least two rolags, if not three, out of one fully covered board.

The finished rolag.

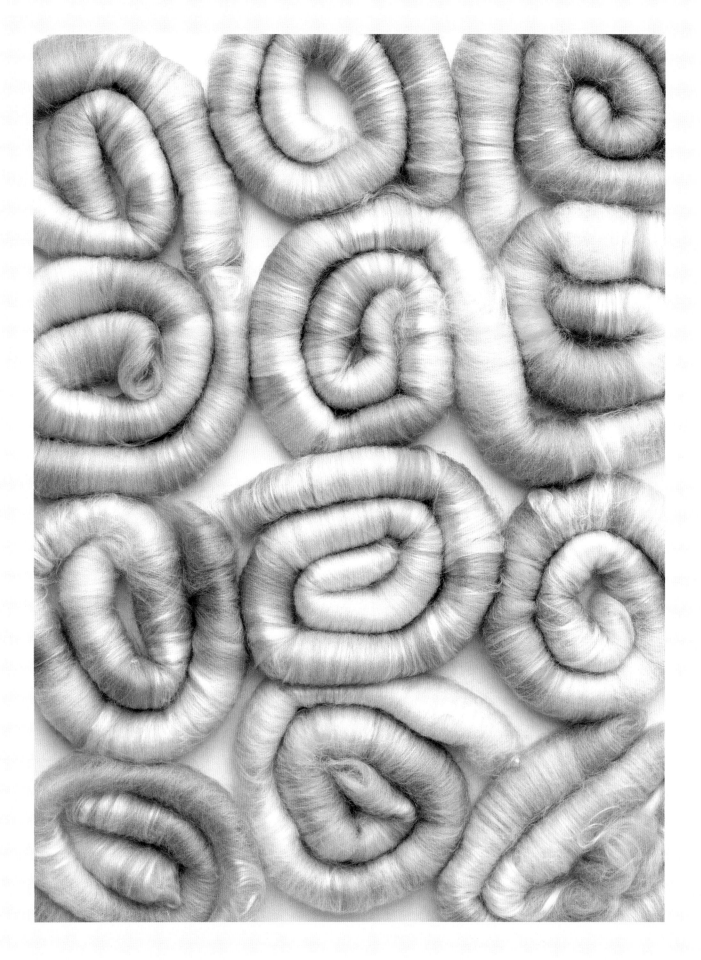

Preparing a rolag for spinning

Spinning from a rolag should be a very easy and enjoyable experience. The fibres are perfectly prepared and ready to be spun.

1 To begin, hold one end of the rolag between your hands.

2 Pinch with one hand and lightly begin teasing the fibres out of the end of the rolag with the other hand.

3 Continue to pre-draft out the fibres to the desired thickness in preparation for spinning.

4 Once you have drafted out a suitable amount of fibre, you can begin spinning. I like to wrap the excess fibre around my wrist while it waits to be spun. This not only helps to secure your fibre from accidentally getting sucked up in the twist, but it makes it easily available for spinning. This technique is often referred to as a wrist distaff.

⇨ SEE PAGE 48 FOR THE SECTION ON SPINNING

Drum carders

A drum carder is a wonderful tool used to card (or brush) fibres to prepare them for spinning. Most people (including me) prefer not to hand card because it is strenuous and time-consuming. In addition, it can be harder to achieve the look you want on hand cards.

A drum carder is more efficient than hand carding, allowing you to card larger amounts at a time. It is best to use fleece that has been pre-washed, because it cards more easily and puts less wear on the machine.

As with other spinning tools, a good drum carder can be purchased online or at wool shows. When buying your first carder, be sure to think about what you will be using it for (batts, roving, blending) and what type of fibres you will be using on it.

The spiky cloth that adorns the drum carder is called a carding cloth. This special cloth is covered with pins and is measured by the number of tines (or teeth) per inch (TPI). This is something to be aware of when you are searching for the right carder. Keep in mind that a lower TPI is generally used for coarse wools and fibres, and a higher TPI is often used for fine wools and fibres.

Drum carders are available as either manual or electric machines. I am fortunate enough to have a jumbo electric drum carder (see below). Fibre batts, as they are called, are prepared as one large 'blanket' of fibre (see opposite) that has been prepared on, and removed from, a blending board or a drum carder.

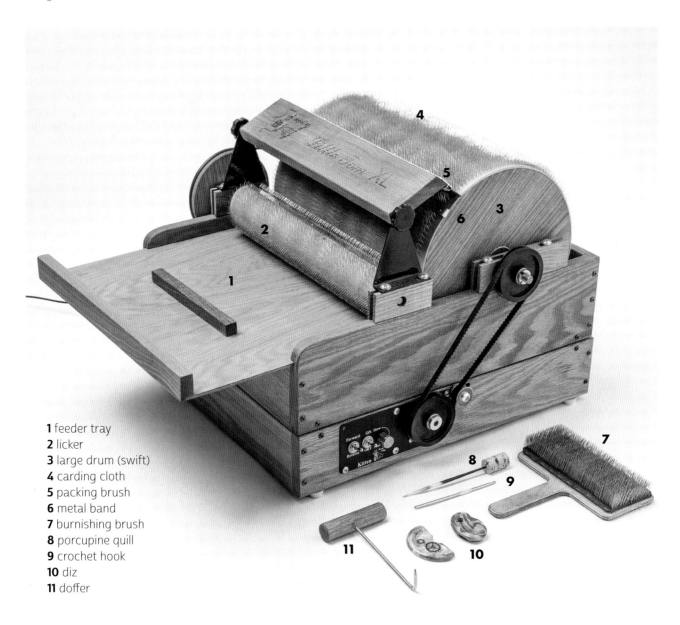

1 feeder tray
2 licker
3 large drum (swift)
4 carding cloth
5 packing brush
6 metal band
7 burnishing brush
8 porcupine quill
9 crochet hook
10 diz
11 doffer

DRUM CARDER PARTS AND ACCESSORIES

1 Feeder tray
The large tray where you can place prepped fibres to be fed into the carder.

2 Licker
The small drum.

3 Large drum or swift
Where you can 'paint' on fibres with more precision when designing your art batt.

4 Carding cloth
The spiky cloth attached to the drums that cards the fibres.

5 Packing brush
A brush that can be angled to pack down the fibres the entire time the drum is being turned.

6 Metal band
This is the safe point on the carding drum to doff (remove) your wool. By doffing here, you have less chance of damaging carding tines or cloth.

7 Burnishing brush
Performs a similar function to the packing brush but as it is handheld you can move it freely and use it whenever and wherever necessary to pack fibres.

8 Porcupine quill
Used to pick small bits of hard to reach fibre out from in between tines. By using the quill instead of a metal tool, you reduce the risk of damaging the carding cloth.

9 Crochet hook
In this case, the crochet hook is used in conjunction with the diz (see below). It is used to hook the fibres and pull them through the hole in the diz.

10 Diz
In this instance, it is the tool used to pull long strips of fibre, called roving, off the drum carder to a desired thickness.

11 Doffer
Tool to assist in the removal of the batt from the drum carder (only to be used across the metal band to avoid damage to the carding cloth).

Right, top: this Spinner's Stash Rainbow Bright Art Batt is an eye-popping collection of hand-dyed Merino wool, rainbow Firestar and Angelina fibres.

Right, bottom: this Spinner's Stash Copper Aztec Art Batt is a crazy mixture of Merino and Finn sheep's wool, adorned with alpaca, bamboo, Firestar, Angelina fibres, tussah silk and flax.

How to create a batt with a drum carder

Creating an art batt (a batt that uses many different colours and textures) using a drum carder is one of my favourite ways to prepare my fibre. When carding, I like to do what is called 'painting' the wool straight onto the drum. This technique is slightly different from the way you would traditionally use a drum carder because, instead of passing the wool under the licker (see page 43), you 'streak' it directly onto the big drum. Doing it this way lets you have more precision and control of colour placement.

1 Distribute the wool evenly across the large drum. In this instance, I want my batt to only be half the width of the drum, so I will only apply fibre to halfway across.

2 When the tines begin to fill, use the brush to pack the wool down. It is also a good idea to spread any small glitter or Angelina across the brush and paint it on the drum, using that instead of your hands to avoid injury.

3 Continue this process until the tines are full or you run out of wool.

4 Lift the packing brush (if applicable) and rotate the drum so that the metal band is exposed and easily accessible.

5 Removing the batt from the drum carder is a process called doffing. To do this, take your doffer and slide it under the edge of the fibre along the metal band.

6 Pull up a section of fibre approximately 2.5cm (1in) wide. Keep the lifted fibre secured in your other hand and away from the drum tines.

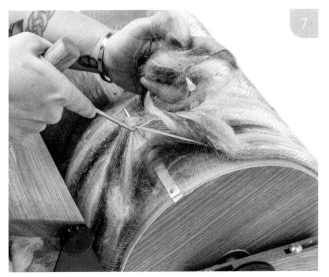

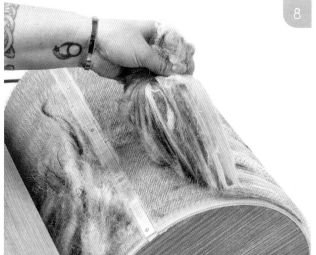

7 Move further across the metal band, using the doffer in the same way to release the remaining fibre from the drum.

8 Once you reach the other side, all the fibre will have been released.

9 Bundle the released fibre with both hands and begin rolling it away from you and off the drum. This will form a roll of fibre.

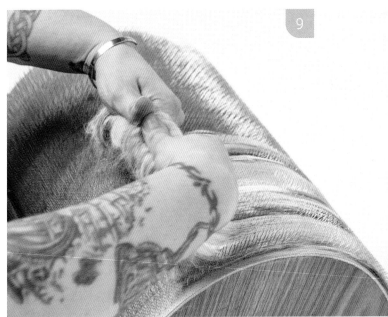

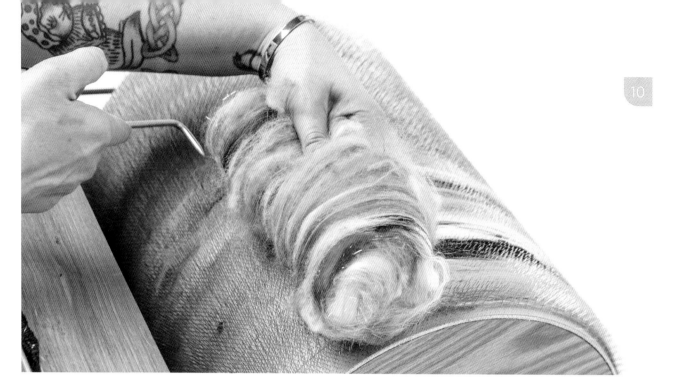

10 More than likely you will have some fibres that do not roll off the drum perfectly. If you happen to get fibres that are stuck, you can use the doffer, a porcupine quill, or a brush to gently lift them off and rejoin them to the batt.

11 Continue to roll the batt until you arrive back at the metal band.

12 Remove the batt from the carder, unroll it and enjoy its beauty!

The Spinner's Stash Monarch Butterfly Art Batt, with carefully selected extra-soft Merino wool, alpaca, fine Firestar, Angelina fibres and a touch of bamboo.

TIP

When you have finished carding (and sometimes before), you will want to clean off your drum carder so that you do not mix in any unwanted colours or textures, and to keep your machine in good working order. You can use the flicker brush to grab excess fibres from your drum carder by brushing in the opposite direction to that you would use when carding. My favourite tool to use is a porcupine quill to gently tease out any stubborn leftover fibres that are hiding within the tines. Make sure to check any gears or moving parts for escaped wool.

WARNING

Do not use the doffing stick to pick out stray bits of wool, as this could damage the beautiful carding cloth.

1 To begin, cut any thread holding the batt together. (If you have bought or stored a batt it may be secured with thread, as shown.)

2 Carefully unroll the batt.

3 When it is fully unrolled you should have a big flat rectangular piece of fibre.

4 Start at the top corner of a long side and begin peeling a strip lengthwise away from the batt.

5 This should leave you with a nice long strip of fibre (similar to roving) that will be easier to handle when spinning. Now that you have a workable piece of fibre to spin with, you can start the pre-drafting process (see page 45) to prepare it even more or you may proceed directly to page 48 to jump right into spinning.

⇨ SEE PAGE 48 FOR THE SECTION ON SPINNING

How to make roving

Roving is one long, continuous combed fibre strip. Roving can be made with a blending board or a drum carder. To make it with a drum carder, you will also need two dowels and a diz (see right). A diz has several small holes of various sizes in it, and helps to turn a big clump of fibre into a narrow strip ready for spinning.

1 After selecting your fibres, loosen up any packed fibres with your hands or a picker. By doing this, you make it easier for the drum tines to brush through the fibre.

2 Begin loading the fluffed fibres slowly onto the tray and, as the drums spin, allow the licker to pull the fibres in. As the wool is carded, it is deposited onto the large drum.

3 Continue to add fibres until you are happy with the amount or until the tines are full.

4 After you have carded your fibre, roll the drum until you see the metal strip. This is a good place to start and will help you to keep track of where you are in the process. Use the doffer to pull up a 2.5cm (1in) width of fibre.

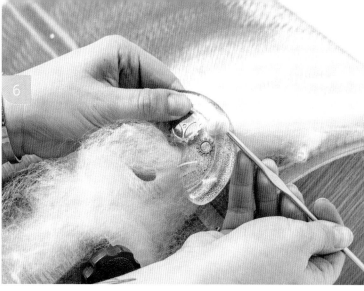

5 Grab your diz in one hand and a crochet hook in the other. Stick the crochet hook through the diz hole from front to back and snag the fibre.

6 Slide the crochet hook and fibre back through the hole.

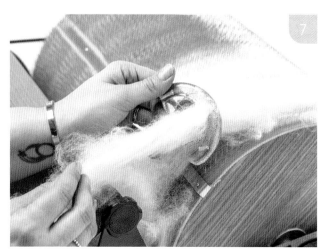

7 Grab the fibres firmly in one hand and push the diz to the base of the fibres nearest the tines. Draft the fibres away from the drum, being sure not to extend past the staple length of your wool.

8 Push the diz back down the drafted fibres to the base of the wool nearest the tines and repeat the process all the way around the drum. The wool should be coming off the drum in one long continuous strip. Once you get near the metal strip, begin to draft and pull the fibres over to the next section.

9 Repeat this process until you have removed all of the fibre from the drum carder. You now have a lovely workable piece of wool roving. You can take time to pre-draft it down further (see page 45) in preparation for spinning, or you can proceed directly to page 48 and begin spinning it as is.

How to prepare roving for spinning (pre-drafting)

Spinning from roving is very popular among beginner spinners. Roving fibres are beautifully aligned and come in long strips, which are more manageable when spinning. Unless you have pencil roving or your aim is to spin a super-extra-chunky yarn, you will want to thin out the roving by drafting. You may choose to draft the fibres while spinning, but it is a whole lot easier if you perform a process called pre-drafting. Pre-drafting is exactly as the name implies – you lay out your roving and draft the fibres to a more desirable thickness *before* you begin spinning.

1 Select your roving and expose the end that you would like to begin working with.

2 To pre-draft, grab the end of the roving with one hand and the rest of the fibre in the other hand approximately 15cm (6in) apart.

3 Ensure that you are holding the wool loosely to allow the fibres to slip past one another. Pull slowly on both ends to separate and thin the fibres until you have achieved the desired thickness.

TIP

Take note of the staple length of your fibre (see page 13) as you will want to hold beyond the staple. For example, if your fibre has a (5cm) 2in staple, your hands should be at least 7.5cm (3in) apart to allow the fibres to slide past one another and give you an easy draft.

Colourways

I get so many questions on how I mix the colours for my art batts, rolags, roving and so on, yet the answer is very simple. I take inspiration from things I see around me every day, from photographs, and sometimes a colourway will just pop into my mind.

No matter how my inspiration comes, it has to be translated into fibre quantities. I generally prepare my fibre mixtures in 100g (3½oz) bundles because this is a good chunk of fibre and 100 is an easy number to work with.

It's a good idea not to have too many different colours when preparing fibre for spinning, because the blended fibres can become 'muddied' during the spinning process. If this happens, you will just end up with an ugly pile of yarn with no distinguishable colours to speak of. To prevent this from happening, I try to stick to about five main colours when designing my batts, because this gives a good variation.

To create your colour 'recipe', select a photograph that inspires you and divide the picture into ten equal segments. I have selected a picture of a monarch butterfly to help walk you through the process.

Looking at the image as a reference, pick out the five colours that are the most prominent. In this case, they are orange, yellow, black, white and cream. Here, I am just focusing on the butterfly, not the background.

Now divide your photo into ten sections using a simple grid. Each section of the grid represents 10g (⅓oz) of fibre. Decide how many grams (out of 100g/3½oz total) would belong to each colour.

Mine worked out as:

60% orange
15% black
10% white
10% yellow
5% cream

I decided to break this up in the following way and use:

50% orange Bluefaced Leiceister
10% clementine Merino
10% white Tencel
5% black flax
10% black Bluefaced Leicester
5% yellow bamboo
5% dusty yellow Shetland
5% cream soya silk
small amount of gold Angelina

The next step is to select and weigh out your fibres according to colour, but don't forget to add in a little texture as well. There are many ways that you can measure fibre quantity, but I just use a set of kitchen weighing scales. It is affordable, accurate, and gets the job done. To use your scale to weigh your fibres you will need your scale and something to hold your fibres such as a cup, bowl or basket. Put your container on the scale and zero out the scale. By doing this you take away the weight of your container so that it is not counted in the weight of your fibre. Place your fibre in the container and record your results. This should make a base fibre mixture of 100g (3½oz).

Now refer back to your original image and decide if there are any subtle colour or textured effects that you would like to add to your batt. I would generally add no more than three additional accent fibres to my mixture, but ultimately, it is your choice.

Add a pinch (about 1–2g) of your accent fibres to the overall mixture. For my monarch butterfly batt, I wanted to add some gold glitter to give it a little extra shine.

Do not worry that your mixture may be up to several grams over 100 as it is likely that you will lose a couple of grams during the fibre preparation process. Now that you have your colours all weighed out and ready, you can move on to the next step in your preparation and blend the fibres on a blending board (page 28), or using hand carders (page 24) or a drum carder (page 38).

Spinning

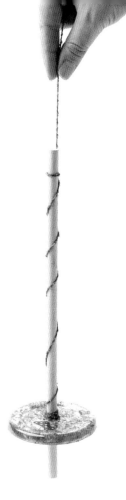

The drop spindle was one of the first tools to be used for spinning yarn, and is the ideal beginner's tool for learning the basics. It is essentially a weighted disc on a shaft. The fleece is attached via the hook and the fibres teased out as the spindle is, literally, dropped and spun. Spindles can be purchased from craft stores and online for a few pounds, and are a great way to spin your own yarn without needing to invest in an expensive spinning wheel.

Anatomy of a drop spindle

A drop spindle consists of a shaft for storing your finished yarn, with a hook on one end and a whorl midway down it. The whorl is the disc that provides the weight to keep the spin going. Drop spindles can be made of many different types of materials. I have seen spindles made of wood, metal, acrylic, plastic, stone and a variety of other bits and pieces. These days you can find a drop spindle with the click of a button. Simply search online and you will find no shortage of spindles to choose from.

The only downside to buying online as opposed to in person is that you will not be able to feel the spindle in your hands before you purchase it. For this reason, I would recommend going to a wool show, a shop, a guild or somewhere you are able to hold the spindles in your hand, so that you can make a better decision on which is the right one for you.

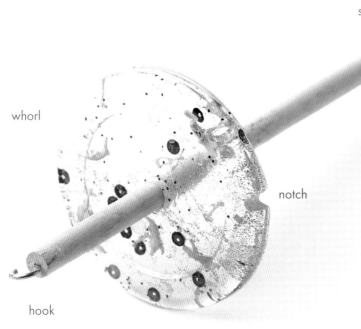

shaft

whorl

notch

hook

Shaft: this is the vertical stick that makes up the base of the spindle and holds the whorl, hook and spun yarn (sometimes referred to as the cop).

Whorl: the disc-shaped weight attached to the shaft of the spindle that assists in increasing and maintain the spin.

Hook: found on the end of the shaft, this is used to secure the yarn while spinning.

Notch: this is located on the edge/rim of the whorl to keep the secured yarn from slipping while you are spinning.

Choosing a spindle

Choosing a spindle is a very personal decision. There are many factors that can sway you from one spindle to another, but ultimately, it comes down to personal preference. The following are a few things to keep in mind when choosing your dream spindle:

TOP WHORL OR BOTTOM WHORL

I have found through research and discussion that there is no mechanical difference to the end product between using a bottom whorl or a top whorl. There is, however, a long-standing dispute on which is easier to use for a beginner. My advice is to try them both and see which one is most comfortable for you. After all, you are going to be the one using it. The photograph on the right shows both types.

WEIGHT

The decision on the weight of a whorl will often come down to two different characteristics: how it feels in your hands and what type of yarn you want to spin. For instance, if you are planning on spinning a lace-weight yarn, you will want something small and light so the weight of it does not break apart your thin spun fibres. If you want to spin bulky art yarns, you will probably want to go with something a bit heavier with enough weight to keep up the momentum of the spin.

Here are some numbers as a guideline only, the choice is ultimately up to you and how the spindle feels and spins.

For beginners, I like to suggest using a spindle that weighs between 25g and 45g (¾ and 1½oz). It is a good enough weight to feel and keep the spindle spinning for a good amount of time. If you are looking for recommendations based on the type of yarn that you would like to produce, here are some useful numbers:

12–25g (½–¾oz) for fine, lace-weight to fingering yarn
25–45g (¾–1½oz) for sport, DK and worsted weight yarns
45g+ (1½oz) for bulky/chunky weight yarn.

Here you can see a top whorl spindle on the left and a bottom whorl spindle to the right.

50

NOTCH VERSUS NO NOTCH

A notch on the whorl is used to secure the yarn from the shaft, over the whorl and onto the hook to ensure the yarn does not slide around while you are spinning. If you feel that you need the extra security while you are getting used to spinning, make sure you get a spindle with a notch.

HOOK VERSUS NO HOOK

Many modern spindles come with a hook at the top to attach your leader thread (see page 52) to while spinning. Admittedly, this does make spinning on a drop spindle much easier, especially if you are new to spinning. If you decide you would like to brave a spin without a hook, you will want to get familiar with a half-hitch knot (see pages 54–55). If you are using a bottom whorl spindle with or without hook, you will want to 'barber pole' your leader thread or yarn up the shaft to the top of the spindle before securing it, as this will help to balance and stabilize the spindle as it spins (see right and page 54 for further information).

BALANCE

You will definitely want a spindle that is decently balanced. If properly balanced, the spindle will spin better and you will have better control over the spin and your yarn production. To test how well a spindle is balanced (without actually spinning on it) you will want to hold your fingers loosely around the top and bottom of the spindle. Give the spindle a good flick to get it spinning. You should be reasonably able to tell whether or not the spindle is well balanced (see below).

If you have no desire to go out and purchase a drop spindle, or you just want to get super-crafty, the option is always there to make your own. There are many instructions that can be found in books and online that show you how to make your own drop spindle, ranging from the highly technical three-dimensional printing, to a stick and a rock. Pick your poison and remember that all that really matters is that you end up with a spindle that suits you.

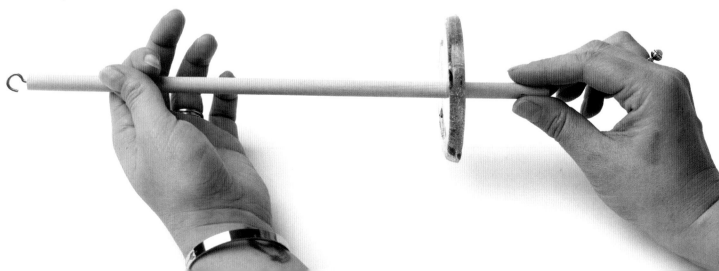

Twisty stick

This is a spindle in its most basic form; a stick or rod of some sort, preferably with a hook on the end. As the spindle spins, it twists loose fibres together to make yarn. When yarn is produced, it bolsters the fibre's strength. One string of yarn on its own is called a 'single'. To make your yarn stronger and more stable, you can twist two or more yarns (singles) together in a process called plying (see pages 68–74 and 86–87).

Choosing your spinning fibre

If you are new to hand spinning, you will probably want to start with something that has a bit of crimp in it or is a little more coarse to the touch. These qualities will assist the wool in gripping onto itself without much sliding, making a beginner experience more enjoyable.

I suggest selecting a wool with a medium-length staple (approximately 9–10cm/3½–4in long) as I find these are easiest to work with. Begin with some wool that has been combed or carded. Carding aligns and separates the fibres making them easier to draft. Corriedale, Jacob, Romney and Blue Faced Leicester are a few breeds that are good to start with, but experiment and find out what characteristics you are drawn to; find a wool that speaks to you, something you think is beautiful and that inspires you – this will help to keep you going when the spinning gets tough.

Attaching the leader thread

A leader thread is a length of yarn that extends from the hook or top of the spindle to which you will attach the start of your wool. You will need to secure the thread around the shaft and up to the hook or top of the spindle, leaving 15–20cm (6–8in) free.

You will want to select a yarn that is a bit fuzzy. The fuzzy fibres make it easier for your loose fibres to grab onto during the initial spin. I prefer to use a closed loop leader and attach it to the spindle with a slipknot. This is the best way, as you can easily tuck drafted fibres through your loop and fold them back onto themselves to make the perfect join.

ATTACHING THE LEADER THREAD TO THE SPINDLE

1 First, tie the two ends of the leader together to make one big loop. Then put the index finger and thumb of one hand through the loop to hold open.

2 Reach your index finger and thumb down to grasp the thread in between.

3 Pull thread through the opening and allow the loop to slide over the thread.

4 Slide the adjustable loop (lark's head knot) up the shaft of the spindle.

5 Gently pull the leader to secure the knot to the shaft just below the whorl.

6 Wrap your leader around the shaft a few times to make sure it is secure and does not twist free of the shaft when spinning.

7 Guide the leader thread over the whorl (through the notch if required) and secure on the hook. Ensure that you leave approximately 15–20cm (6–8in) of leader thread (from the hook) to give yourself space to build twist.

ATTACHING THE LEADER THREAD TO A BOTTOM WHORL SPINDLE

1 Begin by first securing your knot to the shaft of your spindle just above the whorl. This can be done by tying or using a knot as described in the previous section for the top whorl spindle.

2 Next, you will need to 'barber pole' your leader thread up the shaft to the hook. Doing this will provide extra stability to your spin and help to keep the spindle from wobbling.

ATTACHING A LEADER THREAD WITH NO HOOK

If you don't have a hook on your spindle, you will need to tie a half-hitch knot.

1 Use a lark's head knot as described in the previous section to attach the leader to your spindle. Barber pole the leader thread to the top of the shaft.

2 Grab the top of the shaft with one hand. Allow your thumb to slide up further than the tip.

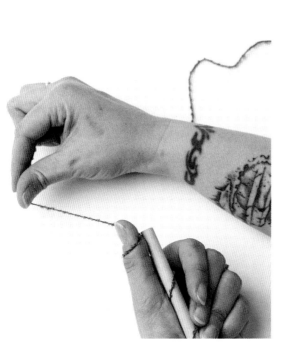

3 Wrap the leader around the tip of your thumb once.

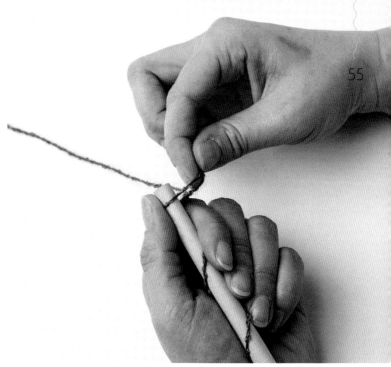

4 Lift the loop off your thumb and over the shaft.

5 Pull the loop tight

6 ...and let the spindle hang freely.

Drafting

In my opinion, drafting is the hardest part of drop spinning. As a beginner you will spin and park your spindle as you go, but as you gain confidence you will want to draft while the spindle is spinning (see page 65), which means you have to be able to draft fast enough to keep up with the rate of your twist. There are different techniques to drafting, but for now, we will just focus on what drafting is and how to get started.

Drafting means taking a clump of fibres (either carded or uncarded) and teasing them apart. It is easiest to draft if there is no twist. If you are finding it hard to draft while spinning, check that you are not allowing the twist to escape up into the fibres between your hands.

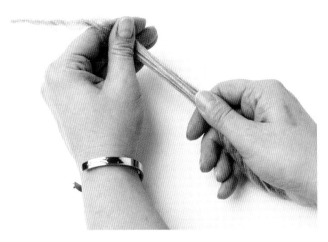 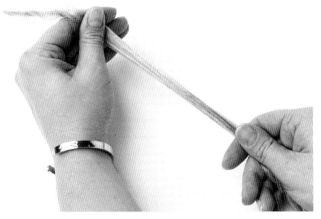

1 To draft, hold a section of wool between the fingers of your left and right hand. Ensure that you are holding the wool loosely to allow the fibres to slip past one another and slowly begin to pull.

2 Continue pulling slowly on both ends to separate and thin the fibres until you have achieved the desired thickness.

NOTE

Drafting 'in the grease' is when you draft fibre that hasn't had the lanolin washed out of it. This is harder than drafting and spinning clean fibre, because it is sticky.

SOME USEFUL TERMS USED IN DRAFTING

Drafting zone
The drafting zone is, as it implies, the section of the wool that you are actively drafting. This section is located in between the wool that already has twist added to it (yarn) and your bundle of loose wool (roving, batt, cloud) that is waiting to be spun.

Pinch point
The point that you pinch just below your loose fibres to keep the twist from travelling into them is what I like to call the pinch point.

Inchworm drafting
This is done by pinching the fibre with your forward hand, pulling fibre from the back hand as you move the front hand forward.

Back draft
This is done by drafting back with one hand and holding the forward hand steady and secure on the pinch point to control the twist.

Long draw
A technique that involves actively letting twist into the yarn as it is being drafted. In other words, you are letting the twist into the drafting zone as you are spinning instead of keeping a pinch point.

Pre-draft
When your fibres are drafted in preparation for spinning. This is good to do, especially if you are a beginner and are having trouble keeping up with drafting while learning to spin.

How to attach wool to the leader thread

After you have attached the leader thread to the spindle, you will need to attach your fibre to the leader thread so you can start spinning.

1 First, draft out some fibres, as explained opposite.

2 Make sure you draft plenty of fibre to get you started.

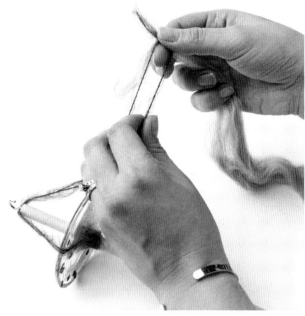

3 Now attach the wool to the leader thread. Thin out about 5cm (2in) of wool and grab the leader thread with the knotted loop.

4 Pass about 2.5cm (1in) of the drafted fibre through the loop of the leader thread.

5 Fold the end of the drafted fibre back onto itself so that the drafted fibre forms a loop through the leader thread. You should now have a nice strong loop of fibres connecting you to your leader thread. The next step will be to begin adding twist for spinning. Once you have decided on the twist of your fibre (see opposite), move on to spinning singles (see page 60).

The twist of your fibre

There are only two directions that you can twist your fibres. One is the Z direction, which is done by twisting clockwise. The other is the S direction, which is done by twisting anticlockwise. General practice is to use the Z direction when spinning a single (see page 60). In theory, this means that anything that has been spun once, has been spun in the Z direction. Yarn is generally spun in the S direction to ply (for the first ply; see page 71).

Remember, this is general practice and not mandatory. If you are unsure which direction the yarn has been spun, it is in your best interest to check. Failure to do so can lead to a devastating unravelling incident. You can check for Z twists and S twists by looking at the yarn and comparing it with the centre stroke of the letter S and the letter Z.

Spun in the Z direction (clockwise).

Spun in the S direction (anticlockwise).

WHICH IS WHICH?

If you find it hard to visualize, you can write out the letters Z and S, or you can hold out your hands in front of you with your index fingers and thumbs sticking out. Turn your wrist slightly inwards and observe the direction that your index finger is angled in regard to your thumb. You will notice that the right-hand index finger angles down to the thumb in the same way the bottom half of an S would. The left-hand index finger angles down to the thumb in the same way the bottom half of a Z would. So there you have it: the righty-tighty lefty-loosey of hand spinning.

Spinning singles

To start off with, you will be spinning what is called a 'single'. A single-ply yarn is what is referred to when it has been spun only once to make a single strand of yarn.

1 Pinch just below your loose fibres right where it connects to the leader thread. It does not matter which hand you hold it in, just try both and do what is most comfortable for you.

2 Allow the drop spindle to hang vertically on its own with no support. Your spindle should now be suspended in midair.

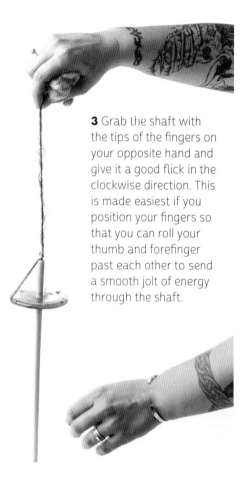

3 Grab the shaft with the tips of the fingers on your opposite hand and give it a good flick in the clockwise direction. This is made easiest if you position your fingers so that you can roll your thumb and forefinger past each other to send a smooth jolt of energy through the shaft.

4 You will see the twist building on the leader thread and you will feel it getting tighter as it spins up. When your spindle slows to a near stop, it means you have enough twist built up.

5 Grab the spindle (I like to grab it by the whorl) and then place it up under your arm high in your armpit. If you are sitting, you can alternatively place it between your knees so your hands are completely free to control the twist and draft. This action is called 'parking' (see below).

Parking

Parking the spindle is when you hold it secure to prevent the twist from escaping. This is done so you can more easily control twist while drafting. Parking can also help to discourage drifting or separating of the fibres while spinning. As a beginner drop spinner, parking is going to be your best friend.

You can tuck the spindle shaft up under your armpit or, if you are sitting, place it between your knees. This will leave your hands free to control your twist and draft.

Starting to spin

Once you have successfully drafted, twisted and parked your wool, it is time to let the spinning commence. At this time, you will want to ensure that your wool is drafted to the desired thickness before you let the twist in. As you may find, drafting will be nearly impossible once your fibres become yarn.

1 Use one hand to keep the twist trapped by keeping it pinched just below the loose fibre at the pinch point. Use the other hand to pinch about 5cm (2in) above that point. By doing this, you are creating a barrier so that when you let go with the other hand, your twist will only enter what was previously the drafting zone and does not escape all the way up into the rest of your fibre.

2 Release the lower hand and witness the beautiful witchcraft that is spinning wool into yarn taking place. The twist will have travelled up and stopped at the upper hand. You will have turned what was previously your drafting zone into yarn.

3 If your yarn is 'over-energized' – spun with extra twist so that it gets very stiff and begins to buckle up onto itself – see opposite. Otherwise, you will want to perform the drafting and parking techniques (while letting the twist crawl up in between) several times. I generally do it until either the twist gets exhausted (at which point I would add more twist) or I have an arm's length of yarn and cannot possibly hold any more. Now move on to page 64 for winding on the spindle.

TIP
To help prevent sore arms, ensure that your spindle arm is lower than shoulder level at all times.

If you create an over-energized yarn by mistake, simply draft more fibre out gradually and let the twist release into the new fibre. This will relax your yarn and relieve any over-twisting.

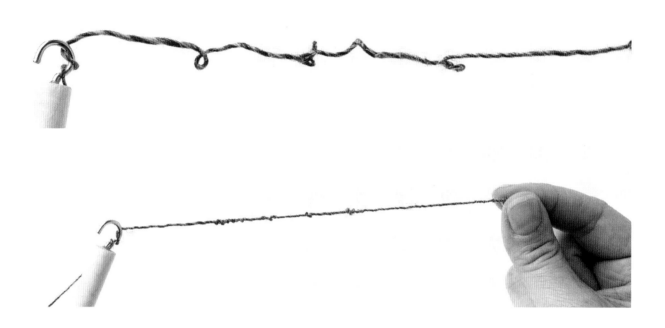

NOTE

If you do not wish to add any more fibre, you can still extinguish twist by letting the yarn untwist (manually untwisting or letting the yarn freely untwist). If you plan to ply your yarn, it is good practice to overtwist it slightly when spinning, as it will lose that twist when spun in the opposite direction. You will find that a more balanced yarn is soft, relaxed and less likely to unravel.

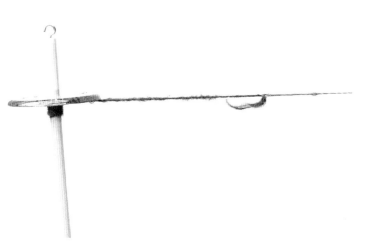

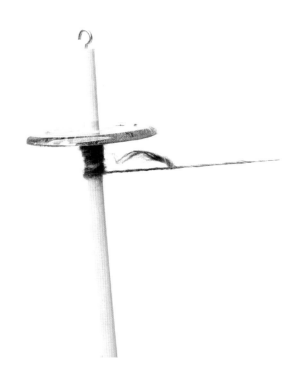

1 Hold the spindle with one hand and use the other to take your yarn off the hook. Hold the yarn out perpendicular to the spindle shaft.

2 Begin rolling the yarn onto the shaft by twisting the stick and allowing the yarn to wrap around.

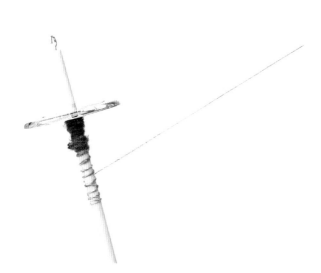

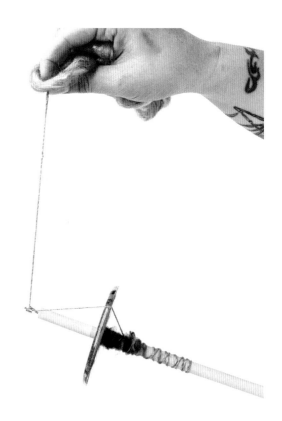

3 Wrap the yarn in a back-and-forth pattern to ensure there is not a massive build-up of fibre in one spot.

4 Take the twisted yarn over the notch and round the hook, leaving yourself enough twisted yarn for a 15–20cm (6–8in) leader thread.

TIP

Winding on in a nice, even pattern is beneficial if you want to later slide the yarn off in a 'cake' – a neat, wound ball of yarn.

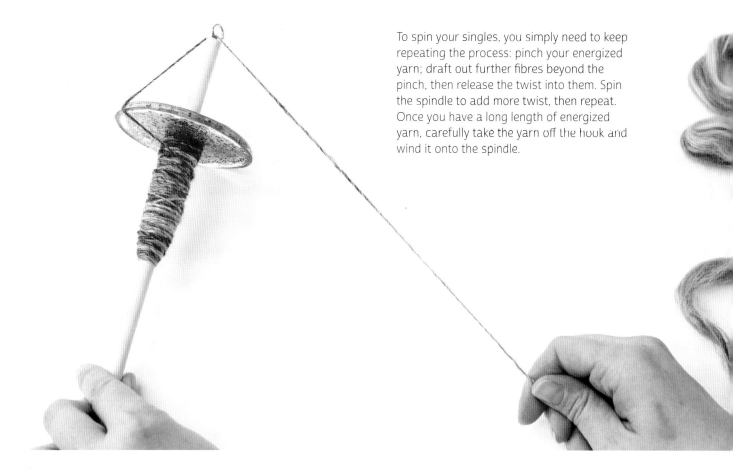

To spin your singles, you simply need to keep repeating the process: pinch your energized yarn; draft out further fibres beyond the pinch, then release the twist into them. Spin the spindle to add more twist, then repeat. Once you have a long length of energized yarn, carefully take the yarn off the hook and wind it onto the spindle.

Drafting while spinning

When you are feeling more comfortable with drafting, the next step is to pick up the speed on the draft, which will enable you to keep up with the speed of the twist. Once this has been mastered, you can graduate to a continuous spin without parking your spindle between drafting. This takes time, patience and practice. You will still need to manually wind your spun thread onto your spindle, as explained opposite.

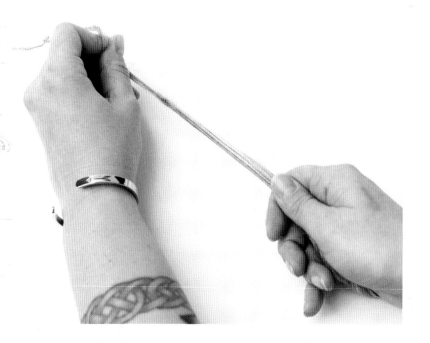

How to make a join

Yarn is just loose fibres that are bound together by twist to make them strong. It is inevitable that you will need to join more fibres for spinning as you go along.

 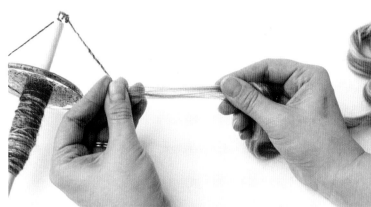

1 To make a join, fluff up the end of the fibres that are attached to your spindle. Fluff up the fibres you would like to add. I generally fluff about 4cm (1½in) to ensure a good join.

2 Lay them on top of each other and draft them together.

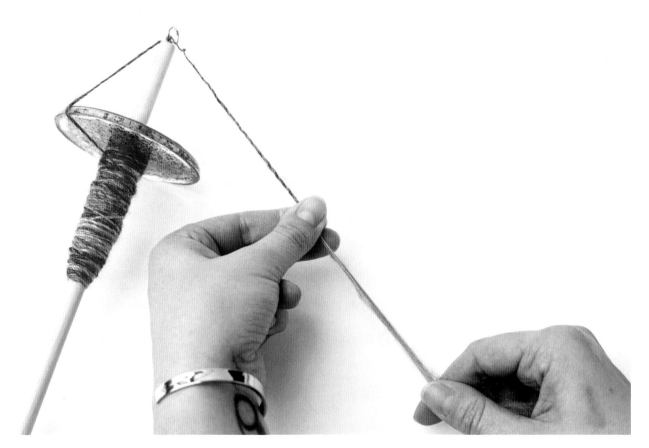

3 Pinch just below your loose fibre and add some twist. Allow the twist to travel into both sets of fibres at the same time.

Making corrections as you spin

It is possible to make corrections to your spinning as you go along. When spinning art yarn, it is often desirable to have what are called 'slubs' in your yarn (see above and page 92). Slubs are points in the yarn that are thicker than the overall thickness of your yarn. However, if you get a slub that you do not want, you can deal with it as folllows:

- Grab on both sides of the slub. Take into account staple length, as this will assist you when you draft your slub out.
- Pull lightly and slowly on both sides to draft the slub out to the desired thickness.
- Release your hold and allow the twist to spread into the newly drafted area. Your yarn should now have a nice uniform thickness.

⇨ SEE PAGE 68 IF YOU WANT TO PLY YOUR YARN

⇨ SEE PAGE 75 IF YOU WANT TO REMOVE YOUR YARN FROM THE SPINDLE

Plying

Plying is done by combining two or more singles together. Plying your yarn not only harmonizes colours and makes your yarn look amazing, it also makes your yarn stronger and more stable. If you need your yarn to be able to withstand weight, pulling, weather and general wear and tear, it is a good idea to make at least a two-ply. This is not to imply that a yarn single cannot be structurally sound; it simply means that if you know you need a stronger yarn, you should definitely ply it.

I first plied yarn on a spinning wheel and the tool used to do that is called a 'lazy kate'. I have often heard a lazy kate built for specific use with drop spindles referred to as a 'spindle kate'. In my mind, it will forever be called a lazy kate in both instances, and for that reason I will refer to it as such.

Lazy kate

The basic purpose of the lazy kate is to hold your spindles or bobbins (generally a minimum of two) to allow them to spin freely as you ply them together. There are many different types of lazy kate available, either via the internet or in specialist shops. The one shown above right has two rods, onto which you put your singles or bobbins so that they can spin freely as you ply them together.

Alternatively, you can always make your own using a cardboard box or some sort of basket. I found a basket that had a filigree pattern and was therefore able to thread the spindle through the holes (see below right). Otherwise, you will need to weigh the spindle down or hold it down with your foot. You will need to experiment with where to position your lazy kate and what is the most comfortable for you. Try putting it off to one side slightly in front of you to assist with the free flow of yarn from the spindle.

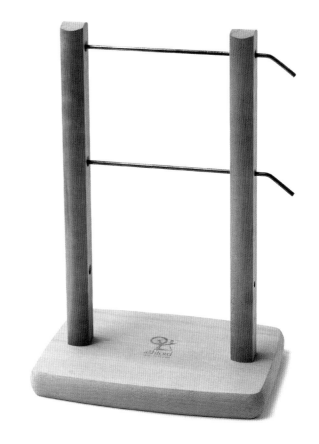

Shop-bought lazy kate.

Lazy kate rigged up using a basket and spindle.

Winding a centre-pull ball

Winding your yarn is a crucial part of being a spinner, and we all have to face that fact that, sooner or later, we will need to assemble our yarn into a workable form. There are several ways of winding a ball and I've found that balls that pull from the outside have a tendency to roll around. For that reason, I prefer to make centre-pull balls.

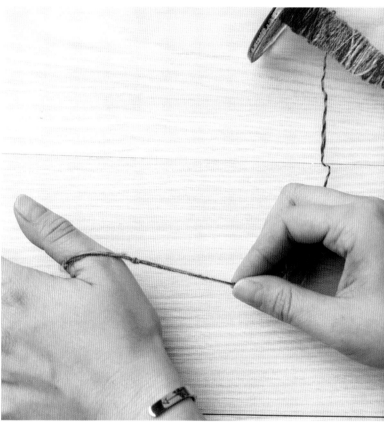

1 Tie a loop in the end of your yarn.

2 Slip the loop over your thumb.

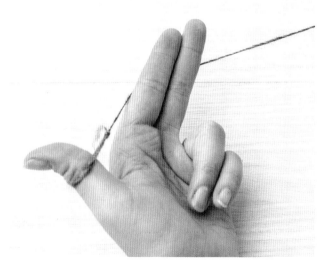

3 Guide the yarn behind your index finger and your middle finger.

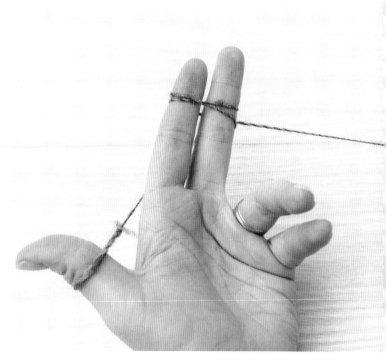

4 Begin wrapping the yarn around the two fingers. Continue wrapping several times to establish a good base to your ball.

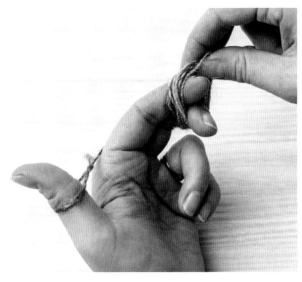
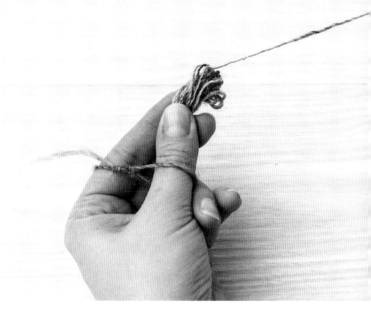

5 After approximately 20 wraps, slide the yarn off your index and middle finger, making sure that you leave the loop attached to your thumb.

6 Pinch the middle to hold it all together and start wrapping more yarn around the middle.

7 At this stage it will resemble a bow tie. Don't wrap the yarn too tightly, as this will make it hard to use the yarn later. Keep wrapping and turning your yarn until you have made a nice round ball.

8 Be sure to keep the end knot of your yarn out the entire time, as this will form the centre pull cord. When you near the end, wrap around the centre of the ball a couple of times and tuck the end of the yarn under securely. Then remove the yarn tie from your thumb, and gently tug out the yarn from the centre.

Making a standard two-ply yarn

1 Put your bobbins or spindle(s) on your lazy kate. Tie the tips of both yarns together as one and attach the joined yarns to your leader thread. In this case I used the lazy kate for one of my singles and a centre-pull ball for the other.

2 Begin spinning in the S direction (anti-clockwise). It is important to spin in the opposite direction to which the singles were originally spun. If you choose not to, you will get a very overspun yarn.

3 Allow the twist to travel up into both strands equally to achieve a balanced yarn. You may want to allow the twist to enter your singles at different rates and angles to produce a plethora of different effects.

4 Continue to spin and load onto the spindle shaft just as you did with the singles yarn.

5 Once the plying is complete, remove the yarn (see page 75).

Andean plying

Andean plying is a style of plying that is used to ply a single back onto itself to make it a two-ply yarn. There are a few reasons why you would want to use this technique. The most common reason to Andean ply on a drop spindle is that it does not require an additional spindle or bobbin to do so. Your hand acts as the yarn holder that allows you to accomplish a one-spindle spin and ply. A more aesthetic reason for Andean plying is that it helps to blend colour transitions by layering and overlapping colours that would have otherwise stood alone in a single spun yarn. But the best reason to do it is that the technique looks pretty awesome!

1 Start by tying a small loop at the end of your yarn.

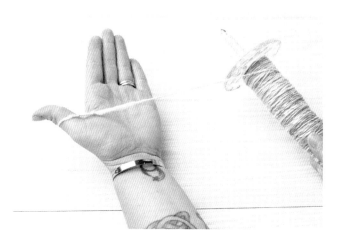

2 Slip the loop over the thumb of one hand and hold the spindle in the other. It does not matter which hand you use.

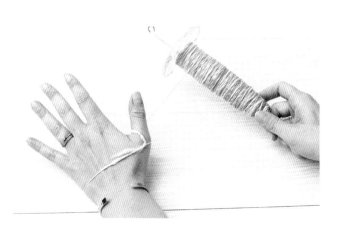

3 Begin winding the yarn onto your hand, but not too tightly. Wrap the yarn from the thumb around the back of the hand, bringing it to the front of the hand from the little finger.

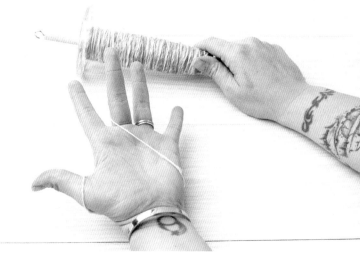

4 Next, wrap the yarn up across the palm to the other side of the middle finger from the little finger.

5 Wrap it around your middle finger and down across your palm back towards your thumb (creating an X across your palm).

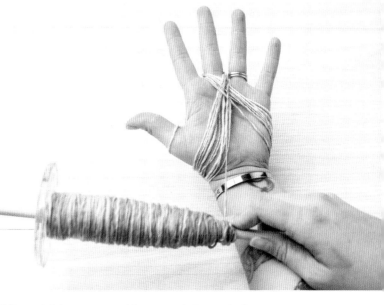

6 Repeat this process until you reach the end of your yarn.

7 Cut the end of your yarn away from the spindle at the end of the leader thread.

8 Slip the thumb loop off and join to the end of the thread that you just cut away from the spindle.

9 Gently slide the yarn off your middle finger. All of your fingers should now be free.

10 Connect the joined ends to your leader thread and spin in the S direction (anti-clockwise).

11 Once you have built some twist, allow the yarn to slip off your hand from both the beginning and end of your single.

12 Allow the twist to travel into both ends of your single to ply the two strands together.

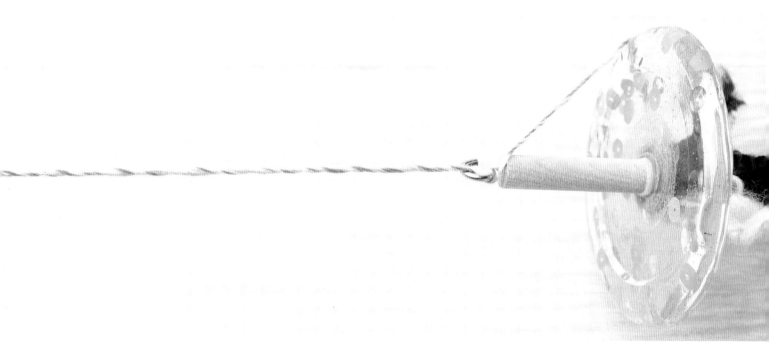

13 Continue this process until you run out of yarn. You now have a singles yarn that has been turned into a two-ply yarn without the fuss of extra bobbins or a lazy kate.

Finishing the yarn

REMOVING YARN FROM THE SPINDLE

Sliding a small cake off your spindle is the easiest and fastest way to clear your yarn (simply disengage the yarn from the hook, and slide all the yarn down the shaft). If you are in a rush to empty a spindle, this is the best way. The downside is that the quality of the cake you end up with is a direct result of how you wrapped your yarn onto the shaft.

If you were in a hurry while spinning and didn't wrap your yarn neatly, then you can run into problems when you try to use it. However, if the yarn was wrapped onto the spindle shaft neatly, you can slide a nifty centre-pull cake right off. The centre-pull strand will be where your leader thread is.

USING A NIDDY NODDY

Alternatively, you may want to use a niddy noddy. This is a very useful tool that helps you to wind your newly spun yarn into a neat skein. You can also measure the yardage of the yarn as you wind, so it has a double function. Wrapping yarn on the niddy noddy is a skill in itself. It is one of those tasks that seems complicated at first, but once you repeat the process a few times, muscle memory will take over and you could pretty much do it in your sleep.

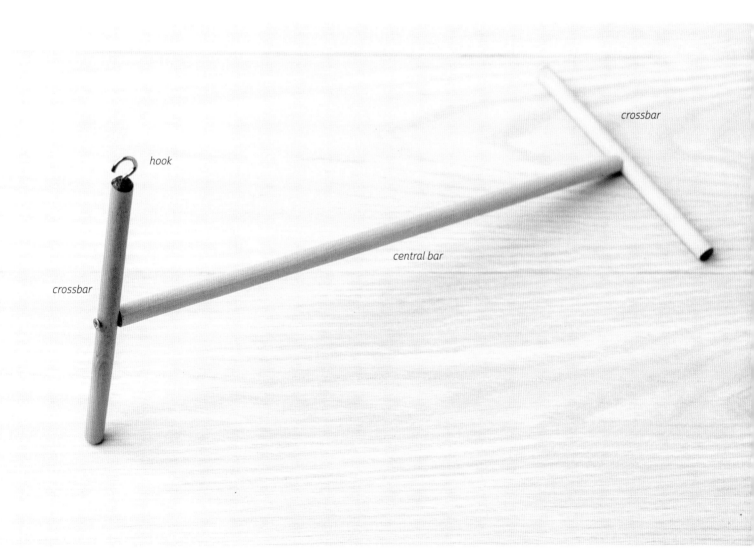

MAKING A SKEIN

To guide you on your niddy noddy journey, it may be helpful to colour code the tool using four different coloured markers, tape, paint or any other colouring material. Add a different colour to each of the four tips of the niddy noddy's crossbars.

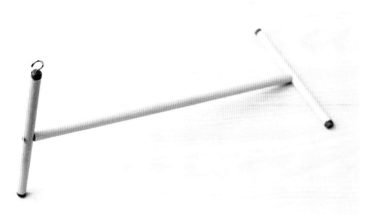

1 I used a marker pen to add green, orange, black and pink to the tips of the crossbars.

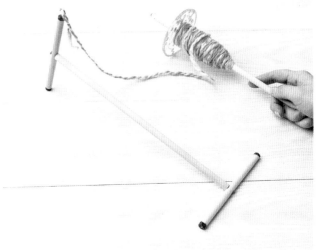

2 Tie a loop at the end of the yarn on your spindle. Attach the loop to the end of the first crossbar, or the hook if it has one. In this case, I have begun on the colour green.

3 Next, trail your spindle down towards then around the next colour (orange).

4 Continue back up to the remaining top crossbar (black), wrap over and head back down.

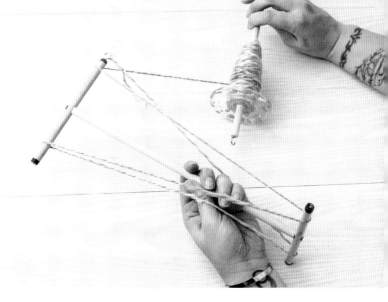

5 Finally, wrap around your remaining crossbar (pink). You have now completed one round on the niddy noddy.

6 Commit to following your colour pattern (in this case green, orange, black, pink) over and over as neatly as you can.

7 The niddy noddy will gradually fill up with yarn.

8 When your spindle is empty, you need to match up the two ends of the yarn. Sometimes these do not match up particularly well, so you may have to unwind a bit until the two ends meet and then you just cut off the excess yarn.

9 With the two yarn ends neatly matched up, tie them together.

SECURING YOUR SKEIN

Once the yarn is wrapped neatly and tied on the niddy noddy, it must be secured. This is done so that when the skein is removed, it does not turn into a huge tangled mess (yes, I have done it, and no, it is not fun). It is best to secure your yarn with some sort of synthetic yarn, thread or twine. You will not want to use wool as this will encourage felting at the fixed points and that is to be avoided. A figure-of-eight tying technique is used at a minimum of four points on your yarn.

1 Split one side of the yarn in two.

2 Slip the piece of synthetic yarn through the middle and cross the strands over.

3 Wrap around the other half of that side of yarn loosely.

4 Tie a secure knot.

5 Cut off the excess synthetic yarn and repeat for a minimum of three more points.

6 Now that your yarn is secured, you can slide it off the niddy noddy.

Note

If you find yourself without a niddy noddy, all is not lost. There are many alternatives. You can have someone hold out their arms for you to wrap on, use the back of a chair, or I have even sat on the floor and used my feet. Just use what you have available and remember to tie some figure-of-eight knots so you don't end up with a tangled mess. Alternatively, if you are feeling adventurous, you may wish to make your own niddy noddy (see page 80).

MEASURING WITH A NIDDY NODDY

This will only be an approximate measurement because of the tension used when wrapping and stacking layers of yarn that create bulk. You may like to count the number of wraps completed as you wind on the niddy noddy but, if you are like me, just concentrate on the winding and then count later.

To calculate the length of your yarn, count the number of strands you have on one side, then multiply that number by the measurement length and you can calculate your total yardage. Example: 55 rounds x a 1.8m (2-yard) niddy noddy = 99m (110 yards).

If you want to measure without the niddy noddy, once your yarn is wound, tied off, and set, place the skein on a flat surface, use a tape measurer or a ruler to place next to it and measure the length of your skein. Count the number of strands you have on one side, multiply that number by two (to account for the other side of the skein), then multiply that number by the measurement length and you can calculate your total yardage. Example: length of skein 90cm (1 yard) x 2 x 55 strands = 99m (110 yards).

Making a niddy noddy

Niddy noddys are most commonly made of wood and built to measure 1.8m (2-yard) skeins. However, they come in many sizes and can be made of many different materials. If you want to make your own, this is how to make a mini niddy noddy for all your mini skein needs:

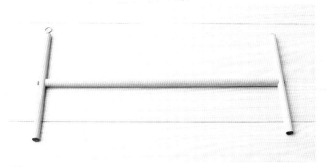

1 Get two pieces of wood, PVC pipe, or any type of sturdy material.

2 Measure and cut three pieces: one shaft of 20.5cm (8in) and two crossbars of 15cm (6in).

3 Take the centre shaft and drill pilot holes in each end (top and bottom).

4 Take the two crossbar pieces and drill pilot holes straight through the centre of each.

5 Lay one crossbar piece on the shaft so it lies perpendicular and the pilot holes match up. Insert a screw through the crossbar and into the shaft so they are held together securely. This will look like the letter T.

6 Take the second crossbar piece and attach to the opposite end of the shaft just as you did in step 5. Now your niddy noddy will look like a letter H (see left).

7 Hold the niddy noddy shaft in one hand, and with the other hand, twist the bottom so that it rotates 90 degrees to an offset position (see below).

8 As an optional step, you can drill a pilot hole on the end of one of the crossbars and insert a hook. This will give you something to attach the end of the yarn to so you don't lose it as you wind on the skein.

If you would prefer to make a standard niddy noddy, use the following measurements: for a 1.37m (1½-yard) niddy noddy, you will need one 30.5cm (12in) centre shaft and two 23cm (9in) crossbars; for a 1.8m (2-yard) niddy noddy, you will need one 40.5cm (16in) centre shaft and two 30.5cm (12in) crossbars.

Twisting a skein

It is unlikely that you will want to use your skein immediately after making it, so it's good practice to twist and secure it neatly so that it's ready to use and in good condition.

1 Hold each end of your wrapped yarn in your hands.

2 Twist one end (it doesn't matter which) several times until the twist covers the length of the skein. Make sure you hold the other end stationary.

3 Once it is twisted all the way with one hand, take the other hand and add two more twists.

4 Bring your hands closer together and you will notice that your yarn starts to twist onto itself.

5 Let it twist all the way up.

6 Open the thumb and middle finger of one hand to enable you to grab the other end of the skein.

7 Pull the tip through the gap, which will secure the skein.

8 You should now have a neatly wrapped, beautiful skein of yarn.

Balancing your yarn

How balanced is your yarn? The act of spinning transfers energy to fibre in the form of twist, increasing the friction that holds the fibres together as yarn. If the twist is balanced, the yarn won't kink back on itself; if it isn't balanced, it will kink and seem to have a life of its own. Here is a simple trick to see how balanced your yarn is.

1 Hold your newly wound skein in one hand and let it hang freely.

2 The flatter your yarn hangs, the more balanced it is.

3 The more it winds up on itself, the more over-twisted it is.

4 So, if your skein looks like a little centre-pull ball, I would say it is a bit over-twisted. To correct this you may need to let it unravel a little – the twist needs somewhere to go.

MEASURING YARN THICKNESS

To measure the thickness of your yarn, you will want to measure the wraps per inch (WPI). This is exactly as the name implies. You can either use any standard ruler or a handy WPI tool.

Hold out your ruler and wrap your yarn around it for the length of 1 inch (2.5cm). Be sure not to overlap or leave gaps, as this can result in an inaccurate measurement.

Count the number of full wraps contained within a 1-inch measurement; this number equals your total WPI. For instance, if you have five full wraps in 1 inch (2.5cm), your WPI = 5.

Here are my suggested WPI for yarn weights:

1–6 WPI:	super chunky (US super bulky)
7 WPI:	chunky (US bulky)
9–10 WPI:	aran (US worsted)
11 WPI:	DK (US 8-ply/light worsted)
12–13 WPI:	5-ply (US sportweight)
14–15 WPI:	4-ply (US fingering)
16–22 WPI:	2-ply (US lace weight)

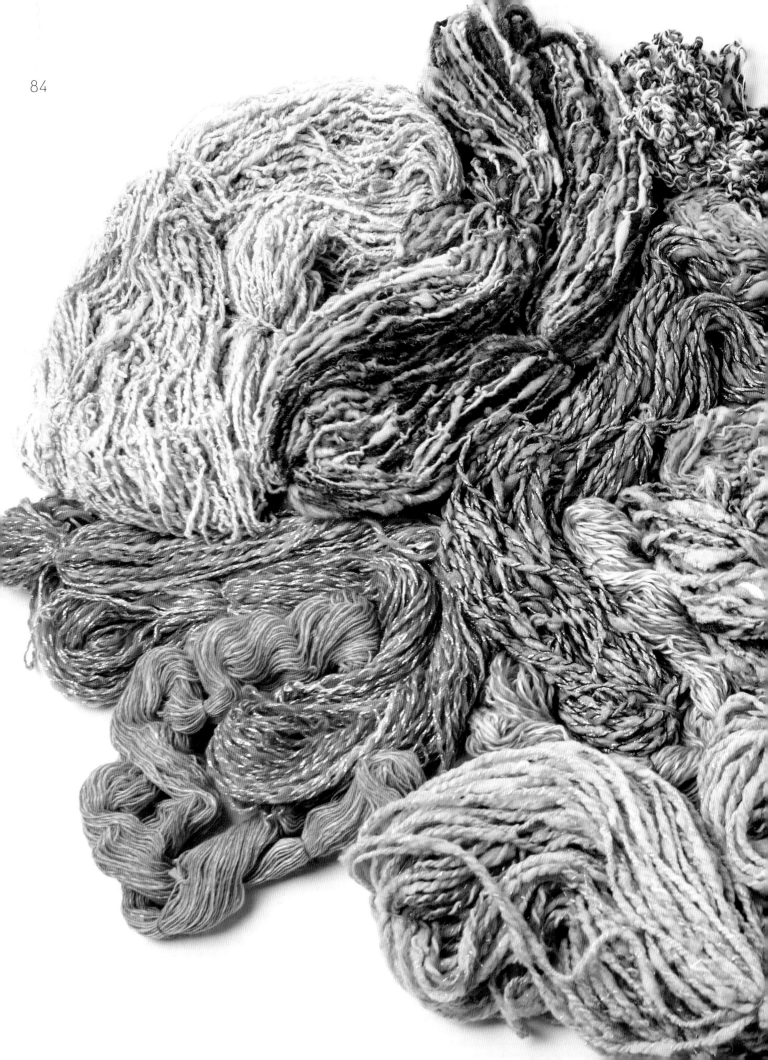

Setting the twist

To ensure that all of your hard work does not unravel and turn back into a big pile of fluff, you will want to set the twist. Setting the twist stabilizes your yarn and will make it easier to handle. There are a few different ways that you can set your twist – it just depends on what you have access to and what type of yarn you have.

STEAMING

Steaming is always preferable when dealing with a delicate or very decorative yarn. Because you are not submerging your yarn in water, steaming will also accelerate the drying process. I generally steam my yarn right after I slip it off the niddy noddy (see right).

SOAKING

For thicker or less delicate yarns, remove them from the niddy noddy then gently lower into a tub of warm water. Make sure that your yarn is completely submerged and let it soak for approximately 15 minutes. You may add a couple of drops of washing-up liquid to the water to assist with yarn saturation. Remove it from the water and gently squeeze any excess water out (do not wring or agitate it). Thwack the yarn onto a flat surface approximately three times in three different areas. This helps to set and even out the twist.

WEIGHTING

I have known people to weight the yarn as it is drying (this will remove some of the yarn's elasticity). I have no use for this so I do not do it, but it is an option

RESTING

Letting your yarn rest is exactly as the name implies. Leave it on the spindle or niddy noddy after it has been spun for approximately 48 hours. It is possible that it will set faster than this, but I find that leaving it on for two days is about right.

TIP

You can set the twist of your yarn with steam or water on a niddy noddy, but if the niddy noddy is wooden, the moisture may warp it.

Drop spindle techniques

Basic thread plying

Thread plying is when you twist a yarn and a thread together to make a decorative yarn. This can be done in countless different ways to produce many different effects. Ultimately, the angle at which you hold the thread to your original single is what will determine the structure of your final yarn. For a simple and straightforward thread ply, you will need a singles yarn, a length of thread and an additional spindle onto which to ply.

1 Try to ensure that the thread length is approximately the same length as your yarn.

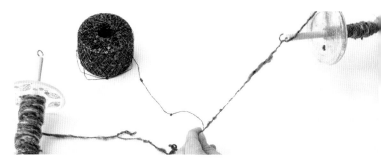

2 Tie the tips of the yarn and the thread together in a knot. Attach them to the leader thread by tying a knot or slipping them through the leader loop.

3 Begin spinning in the S direction. Test out different angles to hold your single and your thread to create different effects in your plied yarn.

4 Continue plying as desired until you have reached the ends of your yarn and thread. Follow the steps for removing and setting the yarn as described previously (see page 85).

Autowrapping

When you spin a single yarn while allowing a thread to wrap around as it twists, it is called autowrapping. Autowrapping can be done in a number of different ways to produce a variety of visual effects. By controlling the angle and tension put on the auto thread, you can manipulate the yarn to create a beautiful design.

To begin, you will need the same supplies required to spin a yarn single. In addition, you will need thread and a lazy kate or something similar to allow your thread to wrap freely as you spin. I used one of my own art batts, called Seal Cub.

Set up your spindle to spin a yarn single and position your thread so that it will wrap freely. I have put my thread bobbin on a lazy kate. Tie the autowrap thread to the leader thread and attach your wool.

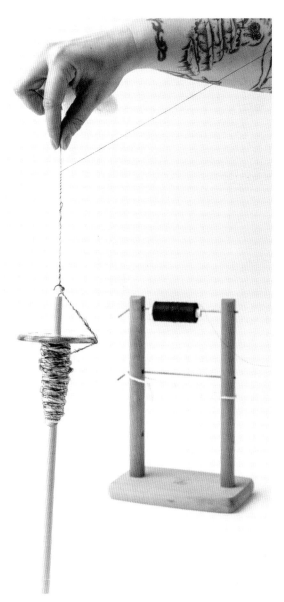

1 Begin spinning your singles yarn while gently guiding the autowrap thread to twist around the single you have spun. Once you have guided the autowrap thread for a bit and established a good secure base, let the thread hang freely and allow it to wrap wherever it wants as you spin and let the twist in. Try angling your autowrap thread at different angles and guiding it to stack up in different spots. You can be as controlled or as free as you want!

2 When you have reached the end of your yarn, remove the yarn from the spindle using a niddy noddy and set the twist (see page 85).

Cloud spinning

Cloud spinning can be one of the most basic ways to spin your wool while still preserving the natural textures. This process can either be done directly after cleaning while the wool is still in its natural state, or you may process the fibres further to create even more unique and beautiful effects.

First of all, collect all of the fibres you would like to use. Put everything into a pile and mix it by drafting and tossing, drafting and tossing (as if you were making a salad). This process not only combines any colours and fibres that you are going to use, but loosens up any packed fibres and will make them easier to spin.

Once you are happy with the mixture, take a good-sized wad and lay it on your lap in a pile (wear an apron to prevent getting covered in fibre). Take some of the fibre in your hands and give it a little pre-draft.

Then spin it as you would any other single. You may have to spin slower as drafting can become more difficult if your fibres have not been heavily processed. If this is the case, revert back to the parking and drafting method of drop spinning until you get the hang of it.

Lock spinning

Lock spinning produces the most wonderful textures and gorgeous yarn by keeping the natural beauty of the locks' structure essentially intact. The process is very similar to the most basic form of cloud spinning.

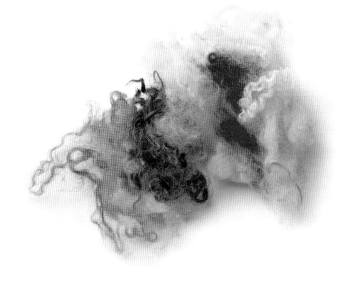

SEPARATING LOCKS FROM A FLEECE

1 Identify a lock on the fleece. Place one hand at the base of the lock and grab the shaft of the lock with the other. Keep the hand at the base of the lock stationary and pull back with the other hand.

2 The lock should come out in one big piece.

SPLITTING INDIVIDUAL LOCKS

1 To separate or split an individual lock without making it go frizzy, start at the top and very gently start to separate your lock into two.

2 Continue pulling gently until you reach the end.

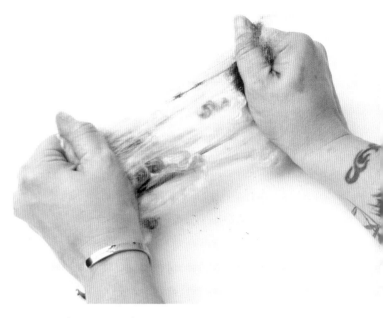

1 Gather together all the different fibres you want to use.

2 Mix the fibres by drafting and tossing. This process not only combines any colours and fibres that you are going to use, it also loosens up any packed fibres and will make them easier to spin. The more pronounced you want the locks to appear, the less you need to perform this step.

3 Attach your fibre to your leader thread just as you did for spinning a standard single.

4 Pinch just below your loose fibres, spin in the Z or clockwise direction to build twist on your leader thread, park your spindle, draft, then allow the twist to travel into the loose fibre. Allow the lock's lumps and bumps to slide past your fingers and twist in naturally, thus creating a very textured look. If you are planning on plying it later, it will further pronounce those textures as they get spun in the S or anticlockwise direction.

5 Repeat these steps until you are satisfied with the length of your yarn. Follow the steps to remove the yarn from the spindle with a niddy noddy and set, or locate your lazy kate for plying.

Luxurious mixture of hand-dyed Teeswater and Mohair Locks carefully spun into a bouncy textured single.

Thick-and-thin singles

These are exactly what is implied by the name: a single-ply yarn that is spun with a thick and thin appearance. Although spinning a thick-and-thin single can look beautiful in itself, generally, it is seen as the birth of an art yarn that will be further plied to create other yarn effects. To spin an easy thick-and-thin single, it is important to utilize the proper wrist action and to use short forward drafts.

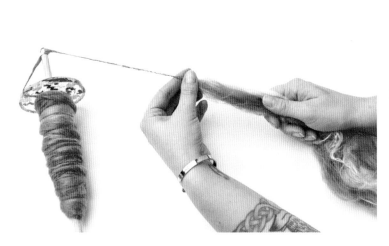

1 Hold your fibre as if to do a normal forward draft.

2 Keep the back hand stationary and begin performing a forward draft. While pushing forward, tilt the wrist down to allow a bulk of fibre to be drafted at once. This will create a thick section of wool with a thin section behind it.

3 The twist will always travel to thinnest section of the fibre. When you finally build and release the twist, it will jump over the thick bit and bind the thin section.

4 Continue to repeat these steps at selected intervals throughout your yarn.

5 Remove that yarn from the spindle with a niddy noddy and set with steam.

Two wonderfully bouncy hand-dyed Blue Faced Leicester thick-and-thin yarns.

Unicorn horn beaded thread ply

Take your plying to the next level and add some beads into the mix. There are a few different techniques you can use to create a beaded thread ply, but I am going to show you the one that I find easiest. 'Unicorn horn' refers to the effect you get when you ply thread with a thick-and-thin yarn.

1 You will need thread, beads or buttons, a sewing needle, scissors and some fibre for a singles yarn, for which we will use the unicorn horn technique.

2 For this experiment, begin by sourcing or spinning a thick-and-thin single (see page 92).

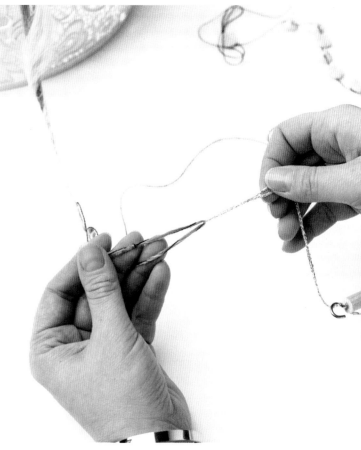

3 Now that you have your yarn ready to go, it is time to prepare your thread with some beads or buttons. Remember, the number of beads/buttons you load now will be the total number used in your finished yarn. To add more, you would have to either break the core thread mid-spin or use a different technique for adding beads/buttons. Take your threading needle, attach it to the thread, and slide on the required number of beads/buttons in the order you would like them to appear in the yarn. It helps if you slide them down closer to the base of the cone to give you enough room to work when you begin spinning.

4 Tie the end of the thread and your thick-and-thin yarn together and attach to your leader thread.

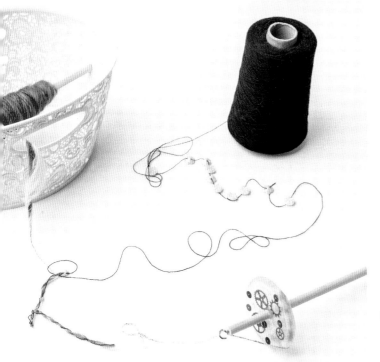

5 Begin plying normally in the S or anticlockwise direction. After approximately 30–60cm (12–24in), continue to hold your thick-and-thin yarn vertical and hold the thread straight out to the side at a 90-degree angle and allow it to wrap several times around the same point of your thick-and-thin. This will create a lock to prevent the unicorn horns from sliding around.

6 You can increase or decrease the intensity of the 'horns' by suspending your spindle from the vertical thread and holding your thick-and-thin at different angles from that thread. Play around with several positions and see what you like best. When you have worked out what you want, it is time to slide up some beads/buttons.

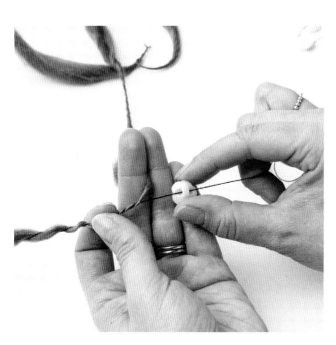

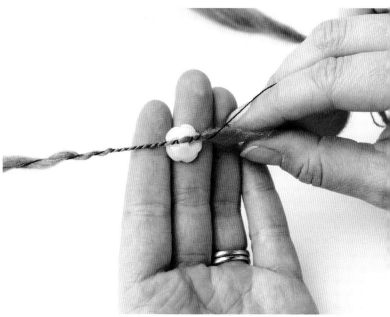

7 Choose the spot you would like to apply a bead/button and pinch there so you do not allow any twist to travel into it. Park your spindle and slide a bead/button from the bottom of the thread up to where it meets the ply.

8 As the bead/button rests against the joining point, hold the thick-and-thin yarn straight out from the spindle and the thread at a 90-degree angle from it. Allow a couple of twists to enter and let the thread wrap around the thick-and-thin yarn.

9 Pinch off the twist again and wrap the thread around the bead/button to make sure it is secured in place.

10 Continue to ply as normal until you reach the next point at which you would like to add a bead/button.

11 Repeat this process until you are satisfied with the length of your yarn. You can now remove the yarn from the spindle using a niddy noddy (or alternate method). Because this yarn has a lot of character that you will probably want to remain intact, I would recommend steaming it to set the yarn as opposed to soaking it.

The Spinner's Stash Monarch Butterfly colourway spun into creamy unicorn horns with a white Mohair core yarn.

Core spinning

Exactly as the name implies, this is when you spin your fibres onto a core thread or yarn. Core spinning is a great way to preserve intricate colourways. To core spin, you will first need to select a core wool. An ideal core wool is a fuzzy one, because it gives the wool fibres plenty of surface area to grip onto. Here are some important features to consider when picking your core:

LENGTH

Any corespun yarn will only be as long as its core thread length. If you would like to end up with a 185m (202 yard) length of yarn, ensure you find at least a 185m (202 yard) length of core wool.

THICKNESS

Since you will be wrapping your wool around the core thread, you need to consider the thickness of the final yarn you desire. If you would like to spin a chunky yarn, then you will want a bulkier core. If you would like a very thin yarn, you will want a very thin core thread.

STRENGTH

Because the core thread is the base strength of a core-spun yarn, you will want to make sure that the core is strong enough to withstand the spinning process. If you find a core that you like, just hold a short length of it between your two hands and give it a light tug. This should give you a good idea of the strength of the thread and whether or not it can survive the weight of your drop spindle (and any additional yarn weight added during the spinning process).

Once you have selected a suitable core, you can get started with the fun bit.

1 Attach the core thread to the leader by tying a knot. Pinch the core thread (that is now your leader) and build up some twist.

2 Park your spindle and keep your twist trapped with a pinch. Lay the fibre on the core thread so that it is at right angles to the core.

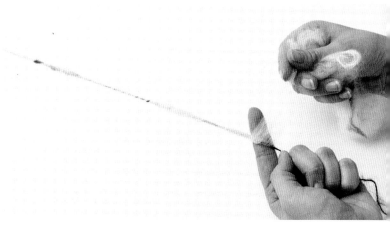

3 Begin sliding your pinched fingers up the core and allow the fibres to wrap around it as it begins to twist.

4 As your fibre hand reaches the core, pinch off the twist while also pinching and drafting out more fibres.

5 Continue repeating this action until the twist has been exhausted, then build more twist and repeat.

The finished yarn.

Beehive core spinning

For this technique you will combine both the skills of core spinning and the ability to spin thick and thin. Using these two methods, you will create the effect of tiny beehive shapes in your art.

1 You will need a spindle, core thread and a singles yarn (in this case we will use a thick-and-thin single on a lazy kate). Take your selected singles yarn and load it in your lazy kate. Tie the tip of your single to the tip of your core thread. Join the two to the leader thread of an additional spindle.

2 Begin thread plying your singles yarn and core thread normally in the S or anticlockwise direction. After approximately 12–24in (30–60in), continue to hold your core thread vertical and hold the thick-and-thin yarn straight out to the side at a 90-degree angle and allow it to wrap several times around the same point. This will create a lock to prevent the beehives from sliding around.

3 Continue to corespin beehives by holding your spindle vertically by the core thread and pinching the thread (that is now your leader) to build up some twist.

TIP

It is best to choose a fuzzy core thread to give your yarn something to grab onto as it spins. This will help to lock in your beehives without having to lock each one in place individually.

4 Lay the thick-and-thin single on the core thread so that it is out to the side at an angle of between 45–90 degrees. You can control the intensity of the beehives by increasing or decreasing the angle at which you hold your thick and thin to the core. Play around with several positions and see what you like best.

5 Begin sliding your pinched fingers up the core and allow the thick and thin yarn to wrap around it as it begins to twist.

6 As your yarn hand reaches the core, pinch the core to stop any twist escaping and slide your yarn hand away from the core to expose more yarn until you have exhausted the twist.

7 Pinch to build more twist and repeat the previous steps until you have exhausted all of your yarn.

Using embellishments

This technique will add a little bit of razzle dazzle that we all need sometimes. You will first need to select a spindle and some fibre. Source your fibres, sequins, bead strips, length of lace, and any other bits and pieces you would like to add (I always think a little sparkle of Angelina fibre is nice!). I generally cut my embellishing strips to approximately 15–23cm (6–9in) long. This will allow a little room at each end to secure them while still leaving enough surface area visible.

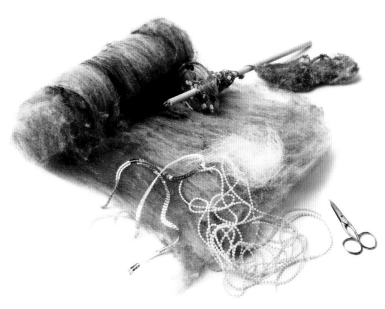

Adding Angelina

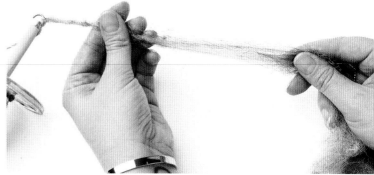

1 To begin, attach your wool to your leader thread and get spinning a standard single for about 1m (1 yard).

2 When you feel that you have established a good base single, park your spindle and grab a pinch of Angelina fibres. Lay the Angelina atop the loose fibres and draft them together, then allow the twist to enter just as you would if you were spinning a single.

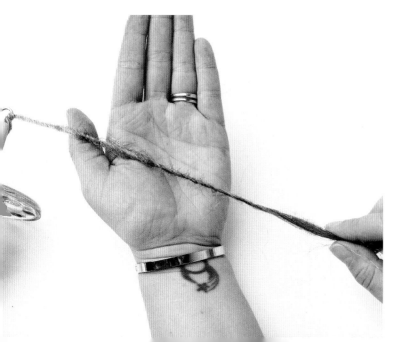

3 Continue to spin the single and add pinches of Angelina anywhere you like along the way.

Pictured right: a Merino Corespun Supercoil yarn with added beads to make the perfect necklace for wearing to wool shows!

1 To prepare for adding sequin strips, remove a few sequins from each end to expose the threads. This will help to secure your strip better and more discreetly.

2 As with the Angelina, continue spinning just as you would for a standard single. When you come to a good spot to add some sequins, park your spindle. At the point where the twist and the loose fibre intersects, split the loose fibre in two by inserting your finger through the middle. This will create a small hole to begin attaching your sequins.

3 Insert approximately 2.5cm (1in) of the sequins through the hole. Be sure to keep an eye on the twist and make sure you do not allow any to escape.

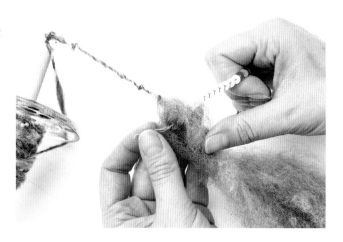

4 Angle the sequin strip so it is pointing in the direction of the spindle.

5 Take some additional loose fibre and use the core-spin technique to lock in the end of the sequin strip. This should only take a couple of twists.

6 Your strip will wrap around the spun yarn so you will just have to untwist that bit.

7 Once unwrapped all the way up to where you locked it in, angle your sequins so they are running parallel to your unspun fibre.

8 Draft out some loose fibre and let the twist to enter slowly as you allow the sequin strip to wrap around it naturally.

9 As you approach the end of the sequin strip, grab some additional loose fibre and use the core-spin technique to lock in the last 2.5cm (1in). Once secure, continue drafting and spinning a standard single.

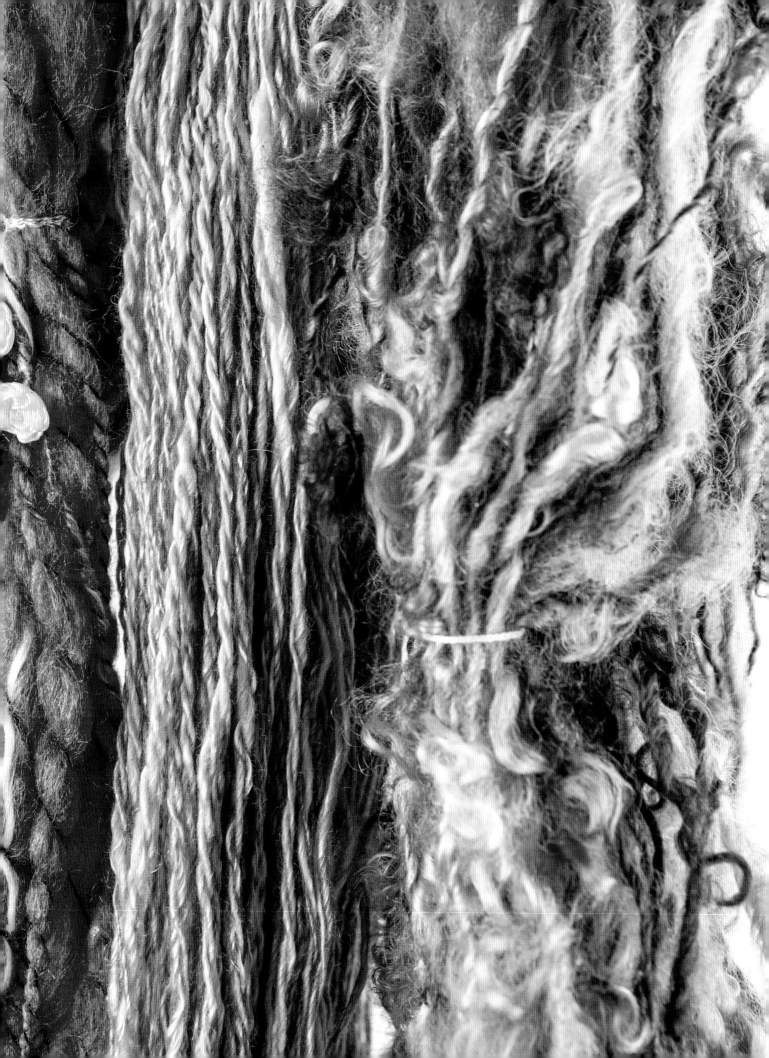

Adding beads

Adding a bead strip is slightly different from adding sequins because they are more rigid. You may want to cut your bead strips a bit longer than you would a sequin strip so that you have more surface area to secure while still having a decent bead section exposed.

1 Begin by spinning a single. When you reach the point where you would like to add your beads, park your spindle and split the loose fibre to create a gap to push the beads through.

2 This is where it gets a bit tricky. With one hand, take some loose fibre and use the core-spin technique to lock in at least 2.5cm (1in) of the end of the bead strip.

3 As you are securing the end of the strip, use the other hand to guide the bead strip so it wraps around the core single and you let the twist creep up.

4 When you approach the last 2.5cm (1in) of your bead strip, take some more loose fibre and again use the core-spin technique to lock in the end.

5 Once secured, continue to spin a standard single as normal until you are ready to add more goodies.

The fruits of labour. An array of yummy handspun yarns in their finished state.

Dyeing

Dyeing gives you the opportunity to add colour and personality to your yarn. There are countless dyes, ranging from natural plant dyes to heavy commercial dyes. The dye I am going to show you here lies somewhere in between.

Acid dyes are a wonderful starting point for the inexeperienced dyer. You can buy acid dyes online, in some craft stores and generally at wool shows. One main thing to be aware of when selecting a dye (aside from the colour) is whether or not it already has the mordant added to the dye powder. Mordant is fixing agent added to the dye to make the colours stick to the fibres. Along with mordant, you will need water, a heat source and a nice big pot to toss it all in. Don't forget to grab some tongs and, as for when you cleaned your fleece, you may find that a potato masher comes in handy.

Acid dyes are generally fine to use in the home, but it is vital to provide good ventilation. Make absolutely sure that you keep your dyeing materials, tools and equipment separate from those that you cook or eat with.

I like to dye my fibre in batches before carding or brushing. You can also dye after your wool has been prepped (turned into roving) or even after it has been spun or skeined. The actual process will be the same at whichever stage you choose to dye, but the outcome and appearance of the fibre will be entirely different.

My simple stove-top dye equipment setup.

Assorted Wensleydale lock bunches separated and hand-dyed.

How to dye fibre

One of the most magical things about dyeing is that it's very hard to predict the results, so it's good to approach it with an open mind! Even if you put only one dye colour in the pot, the wool may soak it up unevenly due to age, weathering, breed, texture and many other variables.

1 Fill your pot with water. You will want enough water so that the wool can float freely. Be sure not to pack the wool in so that the dye can reach all parts during the dyeing process. Heat the water until it starts to simmer then turn it down just below simmering point.

2 Add the dye and let it dissolve. You may want one colour or multiple colours to create varied effects.

3 Add your wool. You can put it in dry or wet.

4 Leave for about 10 minutes to allow the wool to adjust to the temperature.

5 Turn up the heat slowly until you see little bubbles start to pop up.

6 If your dye doesn't contain a mordant, add citric acid or vinegar to fix the colour to the wool. (Use 2tsp of citric acid per litre of water, or 1.5tbsp of vinegar per litre of water.)

7 Leave it at this temperature for approximately 40 minutes.

8 The water should be nearly clear – this indicates that the wool has absorbed the colour.

9 Let it sit for 10 minutes.

10 Take the wool out of the dye bath to cool or just turn off the heat and let it cool naturally in the pot.

11 Once the wool has completely cooled, rinse with tepid water to wash away the acid.

12 Remove from the water, squeeze out the excess and lay it out on a rack to dry.

My typical stove-top one-pot dye set up.

Finished one-pot stove-top dyed wool, laid out to dry on a rack.

Dip dyeing

To dip dye your wool, you will need a suitable pot, a heat source, the dye and mordant (see page 110), a stick or dowel and something to secure your wool to the stick or dowel, such as a piece of string.

1 Start by heating the water and adding the dye powder. While the water is coming up to temperature, secure the wool to the dowel using a piece of string.

2 Carefully lower the ends of the wool into the water, holding onto the dowel.

3 Rest the dowel across the top of the pot, allowing the tips of the wool to be submerged in the dye.

4 Add the mordant to fix the dye to the wool. Continue to soak until the water turns clear.

5 Remove the wool from the water by lifting the dowel. Once the wool has completely cooled, rinse it with tepid water to wash away the acid.

6 Remove it from the water, squeeze out the excess and lay it on a rack to dry.

Other dyeing methods

Using the microwave or oven to dye wool are two other methods of dyeing that you might like to try. They are not my preferred techniques, but I include both methods here, which you can investigate further if you wish

Microwave dyeing

1 Soak the wool in water with citric acid for 30 minutes (use approximately 2tsp of citric acid per litre of water, or 1.5tbsp of vinegar per litre of water).

2 Mix the dye in a separate dye jar.

3 Remove the wool from the acid bath and squeeze out the excess water.

4 Lay the wool on a sheet of plastic food wrap.

5 Use a paintbrush to add dye to the wool. Make sure all parts of the wool are fully saturated.

6 Wrap the plastic food wrap around the wool.

7 Put the wool in a microwave-safe bowl or pan big enough that your wool lies flat without overlapping (this will allow the heat to distribute more evenly).

8 Heat the wool for approximately 8 minutes.

9 Remove the wool and depress the wool with a spoon. The liquid that runs out should be near enough clear; this means that the dye has adhered to your wool.

10 Allow the wool to cool naturally. Once cool, open and rinse with tepid water to remove any excess dye and acid. Squeeze out any excess, then lay out to dry.

Oven dyeing

1 Preheat the oven to 180°C (350°F).

2 Presoak the wool in a citric acid bath (as in step 1, left) for about an hour.

3 Put the wool in a pan and spread it out evenly.

4 Fill the pan with enough water to submerge the wool.

5 Sprinkle dye on top of the wool. Press down gently with a potato masher to allow all the dye to sink down.

6 Sprinkle a little more citric acid on top, to just lightly dust the wool.

7 Cover with tin foil and put in the oven. Allow it to 'cook' for about 50 minutes, periodically taking it out to check to see if the dye needs to be spread.

8 Once the dye is fully absorbed, remove from the oven, uncover and allow to cool naturally.

9 Once cool, rinse the wool with tepid water to remove any excess dye and acid. Squeeze out any excess, then lay out to dry.

Yarn inspiration

KEEP/CRAFT

There is no shame in reaping the benefits of all your hard work. Make something lovely, add it to some weaving, do some knitting, or keep it as is. The possibilities are endless.

GIFT

Nothing says 'I love you' like something handmade. Present your loved one with something they can cherish for a lifetime.

SELL

There are many reasons for selling handspun yarn. Do you have too much? Want to make money? Desire to share your craft? Whatever the reason, display your wares proudly and don't sell yourself short.

Super-thick handspun yarn with an embroidery thread autowrap. The yarn contains mainly Shetland, Gotland and Manx wool of natural and hand-dyed colours. The finished yarn was then knitted into a handbag with a long shoulder strap; the front of the bag is pictured on the left and the back of the bag is pictured on the right.

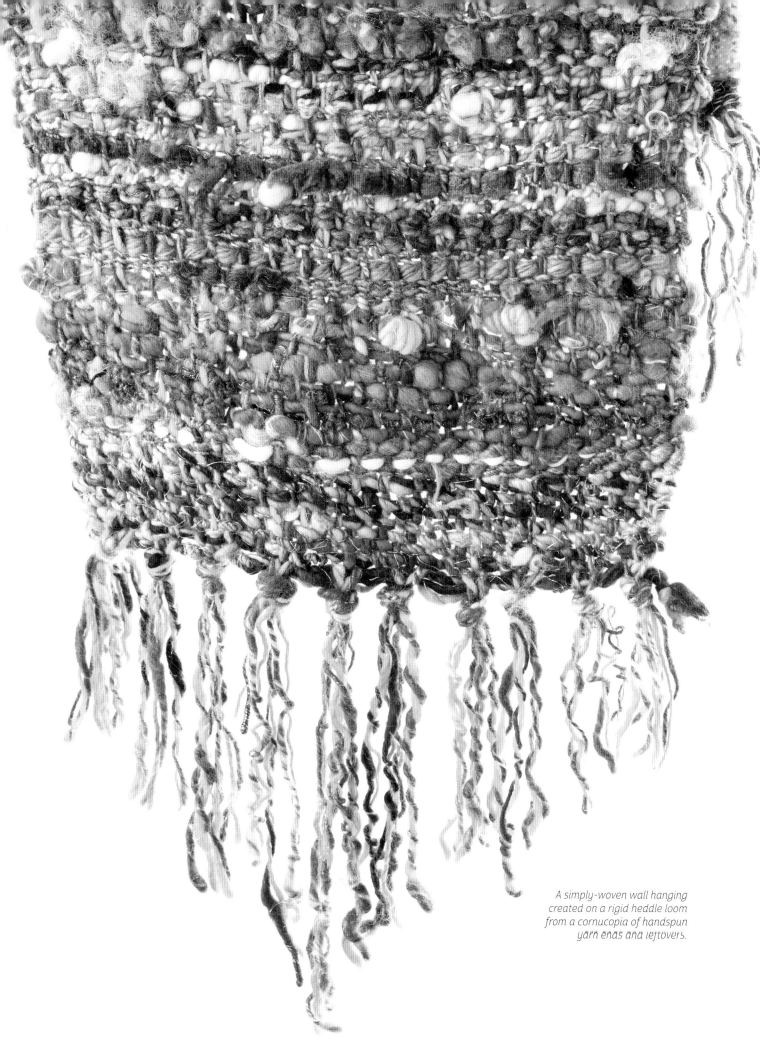

A simply-woven wall hanging created on a rigid heddle loom from a cornucopia of handspun yarn ends and leftovers.

Left: a vibrant two-ply handspun Merino yarn spun with added pastel-dyed mohair locks. This yarn was finished into a long and lush cable-knit scarf.

Above left and right: two gorgeous examples of how leftover handspun yarn scraps can be utilized in other projects. These dreamcatchers were created by Lizzette Mills from Pleasant Dreams Design.

Side view of hand-knitted hood made entirely from spun scraps collected when cleaning the drum carder over the period of about a year.

Above right and left: samples of rigid heddle weaving containing various styles of handspun art yarn.

Beautifully knitted shawl pieced together with handspun Alpaca, Shetland, Merino and Gotland wool.

Opposite: chunky crocheted cowl comprised of a chain-plied
handspun yarn with hand-dyed wools.

Above: hand-dyed Merino spun then Andean plied with a strip of
sequin thread, autowrapped then knitted.

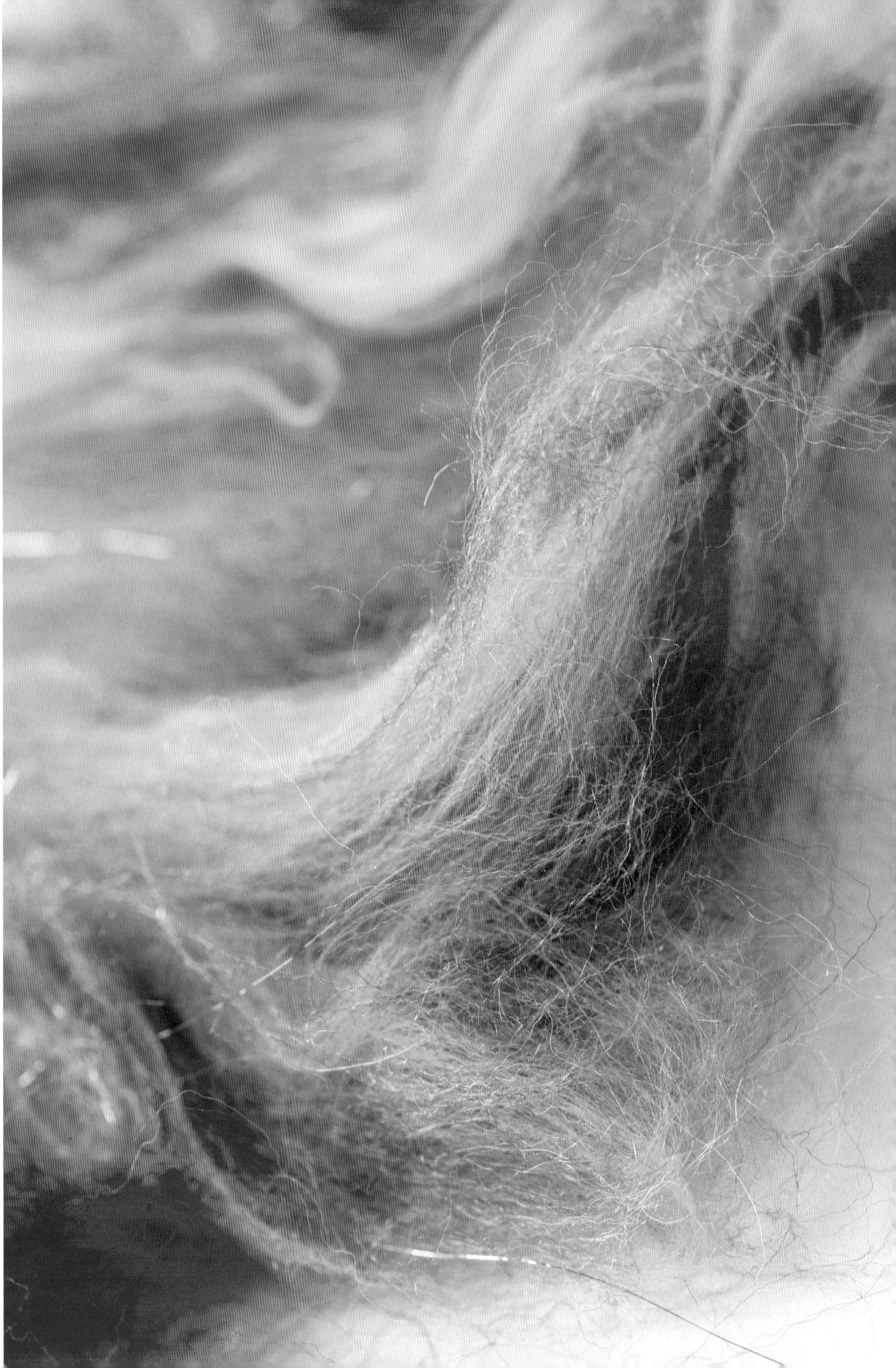

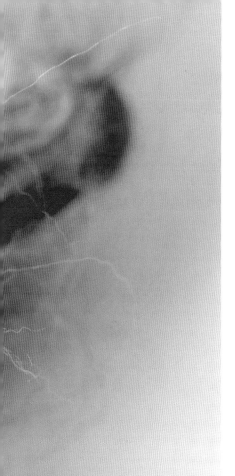

Expanding your knowledge further

GUILDS

These days, you can find both virtual and real-life guilds to join. They both have their benefits, but you can't beat a local guild as far as meeting up with people goes and getting hands-on experience in your area of interest.

INTERNET

Your search engine is your friend. There are limitless possibilities on the internet: you can find books, read blogs, join groups, sign up for magazines and so much more. It is a great way to expand your knowledge and meet fellow crafters without even leaving your home.

BOOKS

Whether digital or hard copy, books are an invaluable resource to learn and gather information on your craft. Cruise the internet, check out your local bookstores, or wander the library aisles.

CRAFT/WOOL SHOWS

These shows are specifically targeted at people who love craft and all things wool. This allows you to meet loads of like-minded people of all experience levels in one place from all over.

CRAFT GROUPS

Craft groups are a great way to meet local crafty people who share your love for making things. You can exchange ideas, learn new things and share your projects while making new friends.

Glossary

Andean plying a plying technique that uses a single strand of yarn (single) to make two-ply yarn (see page 72).

autowrapping a technique used in spinning that allows a thread to wrap freely around a core yarn as it twists (see page 87).

back draft drafting wool by holding the forward hand steady and sliding the rear hand back (see page 57).

blending board a board covered in carding cloth used to blend a variety of wool colours and textures (see page 28).

bottom whorl spindle a spindle with the whorl (weight) located near the bottom of the spindle shaft (see page 49).

carding cloth the spiky cloth that covers drum carders, hand carders, blending boards and other assorted wool-working tools.

core spinning a spinning technique in which you spin fibres onto a core thread or yarn (see page 98).

crimp natural waves in individual fibres.

distaff a tool used to store excess fibres that feed out for the spinning process.

diz an often disc-shaped item, with a small hole in it about the size of a pea, that helps to turn a big clump of fibre into a narrow strip ready for spinning (see pages 23 and 44).

doffer a bent metal prong used to assist in the removal of the batt from the drum carder (see pages 36–37 and 39).

drafting a technique used to thin out clumps of fibre by pulling and separating individual fibres (see page 56).

drafting zone the section of the wool that you are actively drafting. This section is located in between the wool that already has twist added to it (yarn) and your bundle of loose wool that is waiting to be spun (see page 57).

drum carder a mechanical or electrical tool that cards fibres by running them between drums covered in carding cloth (see page 36).

felting the matting together of wool fibre that takes place when the wool is exposed to rapid temperature change and agitation.

fleece wool/protein fibres that grow on a sheep's body.

hand carders hand tools used for carding wool to prepare it for spinning (see page 24).

inchworm drafting a method of drafting accomplished by making small forward drafts with one hand, holding the other hand steady and secure on the pinch point to control the twist (see page 57).

kemp weak, brittle fibres often appearing as the opposite colour of the overall fleece.

lanolin the natural grease produced by a sheep.

lazy kate a tool that holds bobbins and/or spools used to assist in plying yarn (see page 68).

leader thread a length of thread or yarn that measures approximately 15–20cm (6–8in) from the hook or top of the spindle to which you attach your wool (see page 52).

long draw a technique of drafting that involves actively letting twist into the yarn as it is being drafted in long backward strokes (see page 57).

micron count a system of measurement expressed in microns to determine the diameter of the individual fibres or its fineness.

mordant fixing agent added to the dye to make colours stick to the fibres.

noils short fibres removed during the combing process.

over-energized yarn yarn with excess twist (see page 63).

packing brush a brush tool that can be angled to pack down the fibres when utilizing a drum carder or blending board.

parking method of securing the spindle during spinning, allowing more control over twist and slowing down the spinning process (see page 61).

picker a tool used for picking wool or opening locks for fibre preparation and/or spinning.

pinch point the point that you pinch, just below your loose fibres, to keep the twist from travelling into them (see page 57).

plying when two or more singles are spun together.

pre-drafting when your fibres are drafted in preparation for spinning as opposed to being drafted while spinning (see page 45).

puni a smaller version of a rolag, usually made on hand carders.

raw wool the state of wool 'in the grease' before washing/scouring.

rolag a type of fibre preparation created by carding and rolling fibre into easily spinnable tubes (see page 33).

roving a type of prepared fibre that comes in one long continuous, combed fibre strip.

second cuts when the shearer does not cut the fleece in one swipe and has to do another pass. This creates a break in the staple length, so instead of having one long fibre, you have two small ones.

scour to clean or wash wool.

single or single-ply yarn wool that has only been spun once to make a single strand of yarn.

skirting the removal of undesirable fibre and materials from the edges of the fleece.

slubs points in the yarn that are thicker than the overall thickness of your yarn.

spindle kate a lazy kate designed specifically for spindles to assist with plying two or more singles.

staple length the average length of the individual fibres of the fleece (see page 13).

tines tiny metal pins or teeth that cover carding cloth.

top whorl spindle a spindle with the whorl (weight) located near the top of the spindle shaft.

TPI (tines per inch) a method of measuring the density of tines per inch on carding cloth. Lower TPI is generally used for coarse wools and fibres, and a higher TPI is often used for fine wools and fibres.

vegetable matter organic plant materials found in fleece such as grass, hay, straw and burrs.

weathering damage to wool caused by the elements.

whorl a weight attached to the shaft of the spindle that assists in increasing and maintain the spin.

wool batt wool that has been carded and removed from the carder in a rectangular sheet of prepared fibres.

wool comb fibre-preparation tool used to arrange fibres parallel to each other and assist in removing undesirable foreign matter.

wool flicker a hand tool for opening up small quantities of fibres, or loosening the tips of locks.

wool hackles fibre preparation tool comprising a rectangular piece of wood loaded with one to two rows of tines used for aligning fibres and blending colours.

wool locks a naturally clumped section of fibres.

WPI (wraps per inch) a method of measuring the thickness of yarn (see page 83).